Law From Within

Principles of Natural Law

Kenneth E. Bartle

BALBOA.
PRESS

A DIVISION OF HAY HOUSE

Balboa Press books may be ordered through booksellers or by contacting:

Balboa Press
A Division of Hay House
1663 Liberty Drive
Bloomington, IN 47403
www.balboapress.com
1 (877) 407-4847

Because of the dynamic nature of the Internet, any web addresses or
links contained in this book may have changed since publication and
may no longer be valid. The views expressed in this work are solely those
of the author and do not necessarily reflect the views of the publisher,
and the publisher hereby disclaims any responsibility for them.

The author of this book does not dispense medical advice or prescribe the use
of any technique as a form of treatment for physical, emotional, or medical
problems without the advice of a physician, either directly or indirectly. The
intent of the author is only to offer information of a general nature to help you
in your quest for emotional and spiritual well-being. In the event you use any
of the information in this book for yourself, which is your constitutional right,
the author and the publisher assume no responsibility for your actions.

Print information available on the last page.

ISBN: 978-1-5043-0920-2 (sc)
ISBN: 978-1-5043-0919-6 (e)

Balboa Press rev. date: 08/08/2017

DISCLAIMERS

Natural law, being markedly different from *positive law*, has no genre in the literature. *Law in general,* does not suffice. Moreover *Lex Naturale,* is markedly different from *Ius Naturale*, although both refer to natural law as broadly understood.

Positive law, that dominates today, is in most cases Maritime, or Admiralty Law. Within this compass, virtually every english word denoting a member of Homo sapiens species, has been usurped, to include some form of body politic; to denote a legal or judicial entity having that status and obligation. Many words, innocently used in common everyday speech, are deemed, by juristic systems at large, to have a legal meaning overriding common meaning. These include such as person, natural person (versus robot), individual, he, she, and citizen. In the Maritime or Admiralty Law system, for example, nothing remains for any judge to address a living man, or woman. The word *human,* in legal terminology, is not a man or a woman, rather an *animal,* or a *monster*. As commonly expressed, *man is a social animal.*

Consequently, writing, and grammar editing of this book has proven extremely challenging. This work establishes that *natural law emanates from within*—what exactly? Could I use the word *human being,* or the words man, mankind, person, individual, people, humanity, or humankind, without conveying wrongful meaning? More than politically correct, or gender equal, the correct word had also, for *natural law,* to refer to each living being singularly, yet allow for plurality.

The First Book of Moses, called *Genesis* in the King James Version, chapter one, verse twenty-seven, states; *'So God created man in his own image, in the image of God created he him; male and female created he them.'* Accordingly, I have used the word *Man,* to identify all singular living beings of Homo sapiens species, using the capital letter 'M' to denote male and female, within its singular, and plural embrace. For the sake of reducing mental strain, I have allowed the word *human,* strictly in conformance with common meaning; utterly rejecting that *man is animal.* Reasons are given.

Natural law is explicit, and it is immutable. It has no argument with *positive law,* of any variety, because the *primacy of natural law, preempts positive law.* The source of nature, matters little in the long term; God, Creator, Jehovah, divine providence, or energy. *Volitional consciousness,* is the faculty separating Man from all other life forms, animals included, this faculty being axiomatic, by nature. One must use it, in any attempt to deny it.

Because this book, and website at http://naturalelaw.com, disavow the subjects of legal positivism, statute laws, and government itself, neither that website nor this book, infer, offer or give any legal advice whatsoever. This work has no need for the legalese of lawyers, attorneys or (legal) practitioners. Its focus is the study of Man, the orderliness of his activities, his rights, respects, and responsibilities.

All diagrams are by the author, for illustration of idea only; not to be construed as advisory recommendations. All ideas and material presented by the author, are independent from those of the publisher.

Examples used, portend potential outcomes, not actual results. They are not intended to represent or guarantee that anyone will achieve the same, or similar results, since each individual's success depends on his or her intent, application, valued-desire, and motivation.

DEDICATION

To my sons, Craig and Scott, without whose support especially through my near death experience, this book would not have completed.

FOREWORD

On the momentous day of April 13, 1743 the world was gifted with the great Thomas Jefferson who brought with him the wisdom of the past as a gift to the future. There has never been any doubt that his greatest work as the principle author of the *Declaration of Independence* and the third President of the united States stand amongst the greatest accomplishments in history to secure life, liberty and the pursuit of happiness. His life was an inspiration to all mankind. He left this world on July 4, 1826 (U.S. Independence Day) at the age of 83, but his works go down in history as epic.

At a low point in history and in the midst of the Great Second World War in 1942, in a small town in New Zealand, there was born a man with a mission the world had been waiting for to rekindle that same spirit of the past. Little did he know at the time that his life would lead him to such great efforts.

Kenneth Elwyn Bartle was that man; his destiny was inevitable long before he realized his true calling. His career in Australia lay predominantly in architectural design, later researching and specialising in solar housing, but he always knew there was more lying in wait for him. Inspired by the likes of Ayn Rand and the Objective Philosophy, he was determined to find what truth upheld the nature of Man.

The same spirit of the great Thomas Jefferson now lives on in the works of Kenneth Elwyn Bartle and the world will be much better because of it. His works continue where the works of Jefferson and all great philosophers of the past left off. His works aim directly at all peoples of the world, cooperative peace and harmony amongst all men and women.

At the heart of it all are *Individual Rights* (not human rights) which difference cannot be stressed enough. These *Individual Rights* are at the very core of the *Constitution of Man* that is written for all mankind the world over. Until governments recognize these as the primary rights of all individuals no progress towards the peaceful existence of all men can be acquired.

Kenneth agrees on refection that his life has been an eternal search for truth across many disciplines, not fully clear until a recent near death experience awakened him such as never before.

Audaciously stepping outside of common beliefs and practices, there is no doubt that Kenneth's work updates the spirit of Thomas Jefferson, a reborn desire for mankind to live in peace and harmony.

Kenneth offers this work as the truth of *Natural Law—Ius Naturale* as Creator endowed. The foundation of natural law is laid—can Man offer better?

Internet happenstance brought me to Kenneth's understanding, my life has never been the same since and neither will yours.

Max E. Taylor Jr.

—

Further information can be found at Ken's web site: http://www.naturalelaw.com

ACKNOWLEDGEMENTS

Sincere thanks to Balboa Press for their design, publishing, and marketing assistance. Having expressed that this book *had to be right*, thank you for honouring your agreement to make it so in the most gracious, professional and splendid manner.

Thank you Max Taylor for your considerable efforts, suggestions, and edits over the few years this book has taken; your contribution to the *Constitution of Man*, exemplary. Thank you most sincerely for your unceasing encouragements, for contributing the foreword and for your kind words.

To very many other authors and writers concerning natural law or related subjects, thank you for your inspirations, viewpoints, perspectives and focus. To those authors quoted and referenced here, special thanks for expressing your thoughts succinctly and with clarity. Your contributions have greatly assisted my understanding and especially the comprehensive totality of this subject.

Grateful thanks also to many supporters and contributors including my sons, Scott and Craig, also Sian Chua, Ron Hardie, Vanessa Errol, Linda Ray, Richard Yiap, and Diane Knedgen.

CONTENTS

PREFACE

Man's life has been wrenched from his grasp. Rulers, monarchs, despots and religious theologies have built layer upon layer of deception to control the human race to their advantage. This evil assault on the mind of Man has lasted for centuries, and we all are its victim. So evil is this aggression, and so devastatingly effective, it now forbids everything but agreed subservience to state control of every aspect of your life, even in what we call free societies.

Its root is best described by the phrase *Man is a social animal*. Society must be ruled. This notion is hammered into Mans mindset from birth and in particular through the most impressionable years of life. Its toll is devastating. Sociologists, humanities scientists, academia, philosophers, even new-age disciples, indeed almost everyone you meet will all agree that Man must be ruled! So the collective mindset acknowledges state to be indispensable without question, freely votes for it, and fights to uphold it century after century.

So called leaders know what this means. Most others do not because they are grossly misled! Collective ignorance enables sociopaths and psychopaths to invent a fake reality with artificial laws that go against the natural flow of your life as Creator endowed. Governments parasite off the human race while the populace remains completely oblivious of their evil intent. So encompassing and so concealed are their control methods, few even glimpse what life might be, if this outrageous violation of life was removed. People are mostly blind to political evil, and that condition suits sociopaths and psychopaths perfectly. They will do all to maintain mass ignorance, so that (criminal) power over the populace controls their profit at common peoples expense.

Increasing numbers of men and women are reportedly awakening to this theatre of illusion. Sadly, awakening does not automatically prescribe what will eradicate it. Psychopathic controllers do not fear you awakening, rather your certain knowledge of what could and should end it! Reach this understanding, and their game is up. That is their ultimate fear!

Your new found knowledge would smash conflicts, tyranny, wars, and slavery overnight, utterly destroy their money thieving empire and their murderous control of humankind. It would free every moment of your life, smash your emotional traumas to shreds, and turn mental education on its head. You would be enabled to participate in a free society the likes of which you've never imagined.

Two things must happen. First, Man must learn that Creator endowed every man and woman with natural laws governing his physiological and mental functions. Second, these laws are written into every fibre of you, thus are directly translatable into Mans societies verbatim.

These natural laws are Creator's personal invitation to live the most beautiful and bountiful life that you can. They are for your guidance, your fulfillment, your advantage, and protection, your understanding, and absolute joy. Not one of them commands! None instruct! None overrule your free will; indeed one law expressly exists to guarantee your free will! Another ensures that infants can progress in a manner quite similar to adults, despite having no science, no math, and no language!

Creator's invitation to live has never been described in this way, yet its fullness has existed since the dawn of Man. Creator purposefully wrote these laws into our being so that we could discover them, importantly that no one could erase them. Creator left nothing to chance, ensuring instead that you could exercise every free choice. Man's evil has been to deny others freedom and rule every aspect of their life, backed by (deadly) force—belligerently and criminally—to spit in Creators face.

Countless millions long for a free society. Many know that every great invention, thing or art that Man has ever produced is traceable to the initial thought of one individual. Most people know the truth of their individuality and their unique qualities. They truly grasp the importance of independence yet they're trapped. They are mind conditioned to believe that family, community, culture, civilisation, or nation is their life's purpose. They are stymied, fully conditioned to think from a social mindset, because that's all they're taught. Filled with desire for a better world, they are constantly checkmated by the need to conform, register, pay, accept, sacrifice, lobby leaders, become licensed, vote to uphold the state, because, everyone agrees, *Man is a social animal.*

We've all experienced and later witnessed boundless enthusiasm for life in young children, their unstoppable energy, passionate exuberance, and unquenchable vitality. How many have questioned what knocked those wondrous abilities and joys out of the engine room of their life?

This work smashes through the necessity for (top-down) control! It challenges every homo sapiens being to re-assess their exact nature; to consider their bodies, free will, mental capabilities, and emotions. It pleads they reconsider their whole being, as being one that is spirituality beautiful, a finely tuned life-form blessed with incredible potential in any field of human endeavour.

Twenty natural laws govern our being. They exist within you and me so that we can fully function with harmony and precision. If we consider trillions of cells, tissues, organs, systems, mental faculties and emotions as individual contributors to our lives, a new perspective emerges. All of these *individuals* have but one purpose, namely to support your life. All work in their own particular way without interference or conflict because all are governed by natural laws to ensure a cooperative result. They only have one master. Our free will choice.

Think about this. If these same laws were infused into Man's societies verbatim, and indeed they can, what other law could society ever need? None! Natural laws would render every man-made legislation redundant; rules for safety and safe operation accepted.

This approach and its revelations are new—never offered in all mankind's history! Although four years has passed since I began this study in earnest, I am still learning. Many commonly accepted concepts and ideologies are challenged here, including perception, subconscious programming, individual rights, ethics, morality, and justice. Illustrative diagrams may raise questions concerning common acceptance, while new entirely new concepts are introduced including *sequential process, mentoring, and life-values.* My research and findings are founded on Man's nature and his faculties, endowed by Creator as an individual living being. All interactivity and social dealings thus derived, are in complete contrast to *collectivism* as a societal foundation.

Mankind will massively benefit when men and women are recognised to have unalienable right to their life, and that nothing may violate Creator's endowment of life. Life is the base-line reference.

Man is now at the crossroads of his consciousness. Now is time to re-appraise Mans nature regarding individual life, and not as means to prop up the state. It is time to re-discover childhood exuberance, joys, and delights, now to be lived as an adult. It is time to discover Creator's natural laws, to be respected, not obeyed, loved from the heart, where free from restriction and interference the whole world is our playing field.

Your life will change in ways you've never dreamed. Best of all, you will be the master of your life, your destiny, and your soul.

1

NATURAL VERSUS ARTIFICIAL LAW

Blueprints in nature

From the beginning, I had argued in my mind that Mans body is the aggregate of an enormous diversity of cells, tissues, organs and systems, mental processes additional, and that not one of these could disagree with another in the service of one's life. I postured that although all are different, each has only one purpose, namely to sustain life. Every constituent is equally tasked, yet is individually unique.

I sensed that if Man in good health ordinarily, is governed by natural processes that uphold life while permitting free will thought, surely these patterns could be translated into Man's societies. So I questioned in my mind, whether Creator had offered Man a law blueprint within his nature and being. If so, would that be sufficient enough to transcribe into his societies? Would Man need to write laws additionally? Could a society exist that would enable Man's will to run free, yet prevent him from violating another's will to live as he or she might choose?

It became very apparent that no examination of this kind would stand scrutiny, unless it is factually grounded in Man's nature. So I asked myself, what is constant and consistent in Man, while allowing his

1

will to be free? What describes Mans equality with others, but still allows differences from all others?

The answer was free will, jointly with natural law. For Man's will to be (forever) free, Creator must have provided boundaries that would ensure it. So it is that Creator's natural laws allow a governed mental process to coexist with free will, within each of us. This book tells that story. Then it tells how personal life satisfaction may translate into society with no alteration or addition.

I'd sensed that patterns of order (orderliness) must prevail; exactly as Frank van Dun, (Philosopher of Law) describes natural law, from its roots in etymology. If these orderly patterns are consistent and equal in all humans, while free will is correspondingly unique and independent, then natural law most emphatically upholds equality, and uniqueness, jointly.

That connection hit home resoundingly. I totally got it! If the content of our free thought is separate from our actual mental process, then it is possible to have unbridled freedom within a governing (natural law) process; applicable to all! There is no conflict, nor can any be! It is perfect! We are all equal in freedom. Creator has governed Man's mental processes, not to inhibit our free will choices, but to ensure that our free will prevails!

That understanding caught me off guard, but its truth is pure beauty. Its implications have personal, political, and societal application, unlike anything history has shown.

Another revelation struck home. Creators laws and Man's laws are incompatible. One precludes the other. I did not need to study common law, maritime law, positive law or any other legalities. No law library sufficed. I needed only to study Man.

If natural laws govern each of us, then by sensitive extrapolation, they should apply to ethics and morality respective of our social and business dealings. So I sought to understand the full essence and correspondence of natural laws within the nature of Man and his life processes. Results from that study have far exceeded my greatest expectations!

Primacy theories

Did your consciousness or mine create reality and its governance, e.g., the law of gravity, or did nature awaken your consciousness and mine to existence, including its natural rules?

A *Primacy of Consciousness theory,* developed from the works of Plato, Emmanuel Kant, and Rene Descartes, all three regarded as amongst the world's most influential philosophers. Their philosophies remain taught in most world universities. In contrast, more recently, a *Primacy of Existence theory* was put forward by Ayn Rand. Which comes first; *consciousness,* or *existence?* she asked?

These two theories cannot coexist. Look no further for the source of philosophic disparity, non-sensical confusion, and why many people cannot make head nor tail of philosophy.

The *Primacy of Consciousness* theory is the source of collectivism, from which subjectivism has become the psychological and political means to herd Man into states, to rule our minds and bodies, as though we are animals.

Rene Descartes famous statement, *'I think, therefore I am,'* is today accepted by legions as profound truth, such as that consciousness precedes existence. Does it? Consider Descarte's first two words, *'I think.'* Now ask yourself, does the 'I' actually exist? Surely it must, else what enables us to reason? Existence of a conscious mind that can think, shows conclusively that existence of a mind precedes any use of that mind.

Then, the statement should be inverted to read, *'I am, therefore I think.'* Ayn Rand's *Primacy of Existence theory,* bound by that declaration of hers, upturned three centuries of bogus philosophies.

It matters a great deal which of those two opposing ideas one accepts, because it will have a marked effect on all their thoughts, emotions, and experiences in life. This work embraces Rand's *'primacy of existence theory,'* fully refusing the *'primacy of consciousness theory.'* Man must exist for his consciousness to exist and conscious mind must exist for cognitive thinking to proceed. Both are axiomatically indisputable. If ethics, morality, natural law, and justice are our focus, then all enquiry must begin with the existence of Mans life, and his conscious abilities.

Metaphysics

Metaphysics, from the Greek word *'metaphysika'* (literally, *after physics*) is the branch of philosophy that enquires into the nature of existence, our being, and the world of physicality. It is the foundation of philosophy, or as Aristotle called it, *'first philosophy,'* i.e. the subject that deals with *first causes and the principles of things*. Questioning the nature of reality, includes the question—if things exist, what is their objective nature? Aristotle's concern was first the *physics*, then, in sequence, what comes after physics? Hence, *metaphysics is the union of physics with its derivative relationships.*

Sadly that description seldom applies today. Metaphysics is now considered to be external or beyond physics, that may effectively usurp or deny derivative relationships.

Existence, the fact or state of continued being, is axiomatic. Nothing that exists can deny or refute itself. *Existence exists,* is the axiom that states that there is *something,* as opposed to *nothing*. It is present in every thing, circumstance, and event, directly or indirectly available for Man to understand.

Consciousness is the faculty of identification. The first essential of *conscious identification* is that some identity must first exist, or there is nothing to be conscious of, and no consciousness.

Totality

This study is fully comprehensive. Revelations often caught me by surprise. Many times I found need to validate my thoughts because they seemed out of place, even illogical. Many crossed universal acceptance yet appeared valid. Were they or were they not? The further I advanced the more accurate most looked and the simpler they became. Some proved false. Complexities faded away. Supportive considerations offered. Examples became evident. Pointers that suggested a new line of research appeared, and so this totality robustly grew, even though diminishing in complexity. Dots joined repeatedly as the full picture emerged.

From the beginning, I had thought it might be necessary to write a code of ethics based on my findings, if indeed they lived up to my expectations. My greatest delight was to realise that Creator had done that already. Ethics, as a science, is written within the nature of our being. Our individual task is to understand it and live it. Nothing more is needed. That is what this book seeks to impart.

Man's nature, as Creator endowed, is my reference base. Earlier work, assisting my son Scott to grapple with corporatised government, aided by long exposure to legal and contractual documents through town planning and building industry, afforded me a jump-start. Both sides of the coin became abundantly clear. I'll begin with corporatised government and refer to it periodically so that you can also see both sides of the coin.

Government

> If a nation expects to be ignorant and free, in a state of civilisation, it expects what never was and never will be.
> —Thomas Jefferson

Jefferson's words hold eternal truth. Mans freedom and civilised association depend on knowledge, and understanding, whose capacity we all have as individual living beings. The most astounding truth that arises is this, and you can quote me: *Mans individuality is spurned by all the laws Man has ever written; yet is inherent in every law that Creator bestowed upon Man.*

That truth is the most profound issue ever faced by humankind, yet throughout Man's entire history it has been the least considered or discussed. The reason is threefold.

- Societies governments are universally believed to offer indispensable benefits and protections.
- Government panders to that belief and insists its continuance. No matter what good or evil it indulges, it portends to provide essential benefit to the collective. All are to be considered just, moral, and exemplary in the political and legal sense.
- Accordingly, nearly every person on earth believes that government is indispensable to comfort, to security, and that legally regulated society is for Man's best interest. Thus life in service of societal goals is Mans moral duty, to self, family, friends, and the state, no dispute entertained.

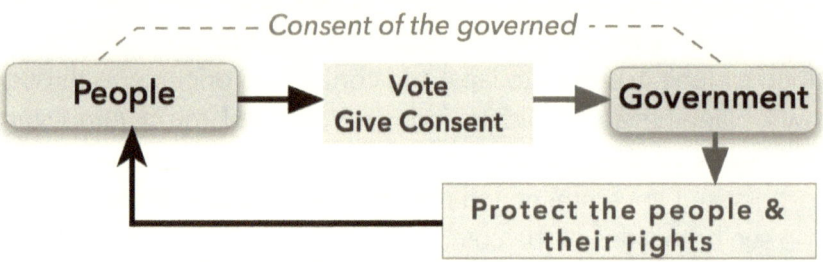

1 - Purposeful government

Leaving monarchies, and dictatorships aside, diagram 1 shows that government was initially intended to protect people and their rights.

Sadly, however, greed, avarice, and corruption, progressively smashed lawfulness based on the *nature of Man*. It substituted legalities based on *society by company*, known today as corporatised government. (This subject is later discussed.)

Laws, as most people understand, are rules written for Mans protection from all who would invade our lives, enact violence, trespass our rights, rob us of our labours, and deny our God-given right to life. Tragically, however, and unbeknownst to all but very few, the *law* they rely upon is not law at all. Excepting for a few elements of criminal law, today's legal structures known as *Positive Law*, widely accepted and obeyed, are fictionally created for political ends; not for Mans freedom and protections.

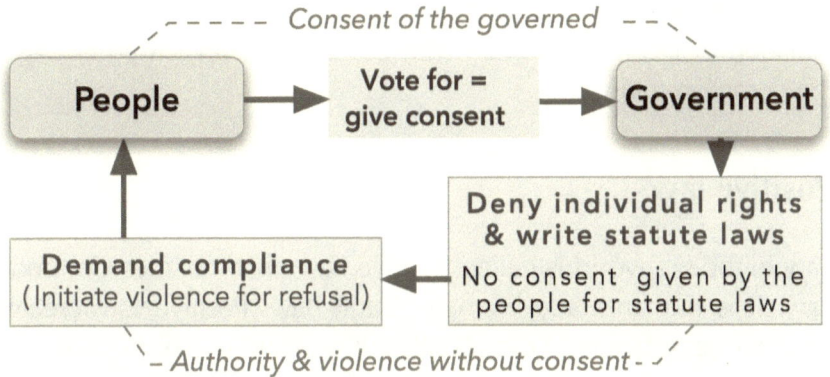

2 - Government domination & control

Government's edicts or laws are (today) taught, propagandised, legislated, and enforced for the sole purpose of maintaining control, including control of Mans thoughts, intentions, and actions. The result is anti-life, as diagram 2 shows.

Observe that the phrase *consent of the governed* is identical in diagrams 1 and 2, but where consent first offered Man's protection at government risk, today it protects the state at Man's risk!

Few people understand this immoral inversion. Today's mindset is firmly that one singular being, or group, has *authoritarian right* to rule others; ostensibly for Man's protection, comfort, and security. So government control is disguised benignly as democracy, wilfully upheld by most citizens. No supporter truthfully admits or confesses to a wilful agreement of tyranny, slavery, initiated violence, and wars.

Thus all *laws* arising from this moral inversion appear, or are taught indispensable to life's comfort, and security satisfactions, and so they repeat century after century, unchallenged.

A conclusion is abundantly clear—

> Any society that authorises a state to rule it by force deserves
> all the tyranny and bloodshed that *authority* approves.

Societal insanity cannot be more plainly stated, I submit. Criminal violation of life will continue with our consent until Man changes the common mindset.

Positive law

Law in today's world is called Positive Law, that includes Common Law. It is human-made, namely statute law. Positive law creates fictional beings called Legal Entities. It usurped our *born name*, by changing its form, then attaching a body politic to the manufactured name. Thereafter, government will do all it can to conceal, that what you think is the real you, is their legal acquisition. Your real identity is stolen; denied. Passport's, driver's licence's, identity cards, and social security numbers are regarded as your legal ID. They are not your ID, however. They identify the *legal identity* created by government, not the living being that your parents created. L*egal entities* are fictions, while flesh and blood living beings are real. Thus statute laws necessarily dismiss and countermand the natural laws of Creator, as they apply to living people. For example, within Maritime or Admiralty Law, there is not one provision, anywhere, for any judge in that entire system to address a living man or woman.

Statutes and directives command us. We're coerced by propaganda and misleading practices, including by the legal profession, into believing that natural flesh and blood living beings are *natural persons*, yet, unbeknown to almost everyone, 'natural persons' are deemed *Legal Entities*. Thus natural persons are not living men and women, legally. The truth is that we function in *positive law*, as and for a counterfeit *legal entity*, stolen from our born name without our consent. In complete ignorance of this deception, we refer to this political fraud as *consent of the governed,* to the utter delight of those who rule us! (Please see Chapter 15 for a full description of Positive Law and its implications.)

Natural law

In his treatise, T*he Lawful and the Legal,* Frank van Dun, Philosopher of Law, writes—

> The word 'law' means order, hence Natural Law is simply the natural order. In the sense in which Natural Law is relevant to jurists, it is the natural order of persons, specifically, the order of natural persons: human beings that are capable of rational, purposive action, speech and thought. In short, Natural Law is the natural order of the human world. Laws are patterns of order. Hence, Natural Laws are patterns of natural order–and, in the juristically relevant sense, patterns of order among natural persons. —Frank van Dun[i]

Please note importantly that in all van Dun's extensive writings on the subject of Natural Law, *natural persons* are distinctly separate from a*rtificial persons*, these concocted by statues or laws within legal systems, altogether, positive law. His work attests that *'natural persons are always living human beings born of nature,'* despite any statute legislation that decrees otherwise, as is the case in Australia.

Law is not what someone said or wrote, whereby all must obey. Statute law is not law; it is statute rule. Natural law addresses the orderly functioning of what already is. (Consider the law of gravity.) Not one natural law commands! All express an orderliness of that which already exists.

If we are to overcome the prevailing mindset that ranks mass subservience higher than independence, it becomes crucial to learn and practice the object of *natural law*, its ethics, morality, and justice. Frank van Dun also offers a reason for the rejection of natural law.

> The practice of Natural Law also has been eliminated completely by the legal profession. Very often, the study and the practice of Natural Law are scorned if not ridiculed. The reasons for this desultory attitude towards Natural Law are many. However, the most important reason for the negative attitude is that the legal profession has discovered that there is much more money to be made from focusing on highly politicised complex, constantly changing systems of social regulation than it ever could hope to make from the study and practice of Natural Law. —Frank van Dun[1]

Nothing is more important than to study Creator's laws governing the intentions and consequences of actions taken by intelligent living beings. Whether one applies conscious thought to any action or not, natural laws will affect the outcome.

2

NATURE AND PHYSIOLOGY

Man's nature

Man's nature offers the only referral base facilitating scientific study of natural law, including for its presentation, application, and education. We are all separate, individual, and unique. Free will is individual, and independent. We are not humankind, as a conglomerate mass, rather an aggregate collection of singular beings. Every man, woman, and child is separate, a unique living being, every one endowed by Creator with all the faculties needed to live his or her life to the full.

Communication between conscious and subconscious mind is the interface between Man's spiritual nature and the physicality of his body, and the material world. This is fully explained later, but here points to a very different view point from that commonly accepted.

Natural laws must accommodate equality, and uniqueness, or they are a lie. Several observations arise from the *Primacy of Existence* theory.

- Every living man, woman, and child, has the faculties necessary for being whole and complete.
- Every living man, woman, and child, is one complete, harmonious whole being.

- Every physical, mental, and emotional faculty of Man upholds life, provided that—
- Man's free will choices also uphold and sustain life.
- Man's subconscious mind is not inert, out of reach, or inaccessible; instead is programmable.
- Communication between conscious mind and subconscious mind, is the interface between Man's spiritual nature and the physicality of his body, and the material world, wherefrom....
- Man is a *spiritual being* living a *spiritual life,* albeit in a material world.

These last three points cannot be underestimated, the last particularly. What follows will fully endorse this idea.

The instant one switches their focus from living a *physical life,* to living a *spiritual life,* is the moment when all life's materialistic nuances, and idiosyncrasies fade away. That idea will progressively develop over many chapters of this book. It will be shown that material resources, products, and physical gains, all prove to be tools (or agents) of spiritual accomplishment, not of materialistic satisfactions, or empire building.

Physiology

The following conditions are fundamental to life as we know it.

- **Plant life is conditional.** When conditions do not support a plant's life, it dies
- **Animal life is perceptual.** Animals perceive food, danger, or a mate, and automatically respond.
- **Man's life is conceptual.** Each of us is made conceptually aware of his or her (immediate) circumstances, and must choose how to respond.

An animal is automatically driven to action by its perceptual faculty. Fear and food (survival) are its primary motivations.

Man's perceptual faculty offers sensations, and perceptions, as it does for animals, but that's where the similarity ends. Man must choose what action he will take, if any. *Volitional consciousness* is Man's free will faculty of being able to think, consider, evaluate, abstract thought, so to form concepts. It does not function automatically. The reason why is very clear—

- Animals adapt themselves to nature, as their nature has determined.
- Man adapts nature to himself, as free will determines.

In his book *Real Answers to Everything*, Australian biologist Jeremy Griffith discusses this difference by explaining—

> —that once our nerve-based learning system became sufficiently developed for us to become conscious and able to effectively manage events, our conscious intellect was then in a position to wrest control from our gene-based learning system's instincts, that, up until then, had been controlling our lives. Basically, once our self-adjusting conscious mind emerged it was capable of taking over the management of our lives from the instinctive orientations we had acquired through the natural selection of genetic traits that adapted us to our environment. — Jeremy Griffith[ii]

Griffith's work confirms the difference between animal and man stated previously. His latest book. *Is It to Be Terminal Alienation or Transformation for the Human Race* claims—

> —that the rehabilitation of our environments and our social and political systems requires a rehabilitation of our psychology, not merely as individuals, but as a species – that a spiritual change must be the basis for social reform and the restoration of the earth's ecosystems. — Jeremy Griffith[iii]

Psychological rehabilitation partly describes this book in summation. Much more offers, however. Its study begins with the nature of Man, but not as an animal. Man must adapt nature to his purposes, but for different reasons than are popularly accepted.

Bodily structure

Our Homo Sapiens body's organise across six levels in a structural hierarchy, from elementary to very complex. The chemical level comprises atoms, that combine to form molecules, then organelles that make the internal organs of a cell. Although we each have nearly 100 trillion cells, they vary in size and shape. Some individual cells may have like functions. Each type of cell has a set of different tasks. Tissues are groups of similar cells having a joint function. There are four basic tissue types, each comprising two different types of cells. Each tissue has an essential role within the body. Organs consist of at least two different tissue types, each performing a particular task within the body. One or more organs work together to accomplish a common system-purpose, such as the Cardiovascular System, in which heart and blood vessels work together to circulate blood throughout the body, so as to provide oxygen and nutrients to cells. The organisational level is highest, being all structural levels working together, or the being (or organism) as a whole.

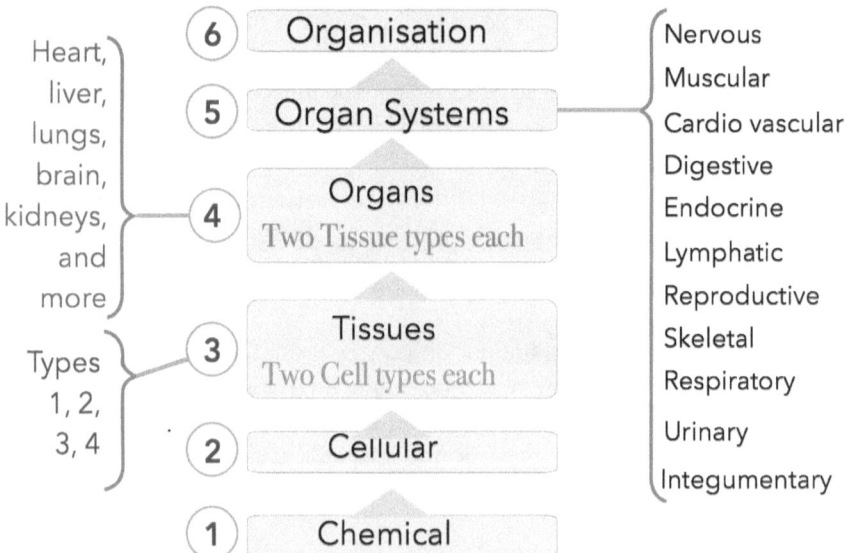

3 - Orderly patterns

Diagram 3 shows orderliness of development, from cells, to tissues, to organs. Importantly it shows patterns of order that govern functioning, namely, natural laws. How could one's cardiovascular system possibly work without addressing its reality, self-honesty, purpose, and integrity, for example? It could not. Neither could any of Mans other systems function outside self-sustaining ethical boundaries. Every cell, bone, organ, system, and function that is within Mans body, must perform within its Natural Laws. Otherwise, it will fail, thereby influencing other organs or systems to cease functioning.

It is evident from the diagram that Creator has used patterns of internal order, congruence, interdependence, interoperability, harmony, systematisation, and sequence. Thus for the human organism, life is Mans purpose, means, function, and goal. That kind of orderliness precisely echoes what Frank van Dun describes as *Natural Law*.

Physiology as concerns Natural Law

Individual uniqueness and *natural laws* that we share equally, and in common, are entirely modelled by Creator right within our body and mental structures. They speak of method, system, logic, process, order, equality, and harmonious cooperation. Man cannot write this law. It is already written within you and me.

No accident of nature, this is evidence of a master plan that science and human sciences should have examined and learned from aeons ago, so as to model society on these natural laws.

This raises the question as to how our body, or mental systems, might be able to track staggering amounts of data, having respect to overseeing and governing all body systems, organs, muscles, and functions. Think of the way in which a factory manages processes, then consider these examples—

- Your body produces twenty-five million new cells each second.

- Our brains use twenty percent of the entire body's oxygen and calorie intake, despite only accounting for about two percent of an adult's body mass.
- The focusing muscles in your eyes move around 100,000 times a day. To give your leg muscles the same workout, you'd need to walk fifty miles.
- A single human sperm contains the 37.5mb of male DNA. That means an average man's ejaculation sees the transfer of 1500 terabytes of information.
- Nerve impulses travel to and from the brain at speeds of up to 250 miles per hour.
- If the homo sapiens brain were a computer, it could perform thirty-eight thousand, trillion operations per second. The world's most powerful supercomputer is flat pressed to manage .002% of that.

Five senses

Aristotle, (384 BC—322 BC), is the recognised author of classification of the five sense organs: sight, smell, taste, touch, and hearing. These represent the interface between Mans body and mental processes, and the real word external environment in which he lives. Although humans are considered to have fifteen other senses, I'll refer only to the five senses with which most people are familiar.

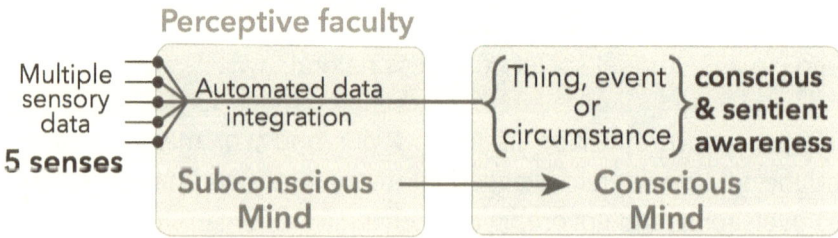

4 - Perceptive process

Our perceptual faculty, (perception), is an integrative process of the subconscious mind. Our being consciously aware of something, our perceiving of a thing, is the (identifying) process of our conscious mind. Recognising the existence of a thing, event, or circumstance, is very different from comprehending exactly what it is, what its properties are, what its purpose or value may be.

The distinction between *awareness* and *understanding* is vital, because it shows that neither perception, perceiving, or conscious awareness, informs full information about what we perceive, or of what we are consciously aware.

The fundamental purpose of Mans intellect is to grasp the truth. Just as one's eyes seek light, so mind seeks the truth, thus to possess it. It desires agreement of itself with a thing, or event, because truthfulness is fidelity to one's life, necessary to uphold it.

Intellect is the faculty of reasoning, of understanding objectively, especially about matters that are abstract. Intellect is also the capacity for thinking, and reasoning, as distinct from feeling or wishing. It is also the ability to learn and reason; one's capacity for knowledge and understanding.

Some mental processes are what we might call automatic, while other processes result from our free will intention. Thoughts are not automatic. We must *will* thoughts into being. Thus we are blessed with two mental attributes or tools.

- **Intelligence** is the intellectual ability to *recognise self-evident truths*.
- **Reason**, is the mental ability to logically think through connected steps, *in search of truth that is not self-evident*.

Unfortunately, vocabulary has today become pliable; often bent or disguised to suit a particular purpose. Texting, and political correctness qualify as chief offenders. I make this point so as to caution readers to be alert. Just as reasoning is not interchangeable with intelligence, so it will be seen that many following concepts have precise meanings, for resolute understanding.

3

MENTAL FACULTIES

Awareness and Perception

Perception, (from the Latin *perceptio, percipio*), is defined as the organisation, identification, and interpretation of sensory information, in order to represent and understand our environment. Many other descriptions and definitions can be found. Mental confusion rules the day, which leaves one vital question.

Is perception a *mental process*, or is it the *outcome of a mental process*? The answer to that question has vital importance.

Animals, and humans, have a perceptive faculty. Its task is to integrate sensory data such as lines, textures, surfaces, planes, curves, colours, and even smell, touch, or taste; so as to present one thing, event, or circumstance, to one's conscious mind; i.e. to our conscious awareness. So when we speak of perceiving something, what we're saying is that we're consciously aware of that thing. We're witnessing the result of a process, which the perceptive faculty has already performed automatically. We're conscious of a particular entity, or event, the sum of multiple data integrated into a whole, not a haphazard jumble of unrelated sensory data.

Awareness vs Understanding

Awareness, perception, and sentience comprise the three elements that prompt our conscious cognitive processes.

- Perception, as a (part) faculty of subconscious mind, makes available the conscious recognition of a thing, or event, which prior was nothing but an unrecognisable jumble of sensory stimuli.
- Perception makes us consciously aware. Perception is the end product of the automated perceptual process, therefore. Thereafter, it necessarily ceases.
- Free will can now work freely and independently. Cognitive thinking develops an understanding of the thing, event, or circumstance, with full freedom to explore every avenue in search of truthfulness.

All knowledge comes from and through our automatic (perception) interface. It is Mans authentic and accurate access to raw information concerning his environment and his world, but not his understanding of it. It is possible for example, to walk into a factory, or science laboratory, to see and become consciously aware of many different objects, and things, yet have no knowledge of what they are, what material they're from, or what purpose they serve. Nonetheless, one sees integrated whole things, not a haphazard assortment of sensory stimuli. The faculty of perception has automatically condensed a multiplicity of sensory information. We are made consciously aware of particular objects, or things.

Sad too say, many people confuse *conscious awareness* with *cognitive understanding*. Far too many people use the words *awareness*, *perception*, and *understanding*, as though all mean the same thing. This is probably the greatest and most debilitating short circuit of one's mental faculties possible. Meaning is diluted as a result.

Nothing teaches that perception is a *subconscious process*, while *awareness* is its product in the *conscious mind*, moreover that cognitive understanding can only result from free will enquiry. *Process* is confused with *product*, while the roles of our conscious and subconscious mind are hidden.

Clear understanding becomes imperative.

- For an animal, awareness, results from perception of a condition, or event, *absent cognitive understanding*, precisely because it lacks that mental faculty.
- Man is differently equipped. To be aware, is to consciously recognise a condition, or event. This *prompts a process of investigation and evaluation*, which usually leads to *cognitive understanding*; being what no animal can ever grasp.

For the same witnessed event, an animal is *perceptively aware*, while Man is made *consciously aware*. Lessons emerge for our understanding;

- *Perception is automatically delivered as truthful,* because it is an (image) statement of concretised existence.
- *Conscious understanding is open to error.* It results from an investigative process willed by choice.

Sentient Consciousness

Sentience is sensory ability to feel, or perceive of a feeling. Sentient consciousness means conscious awareness of one's feelings, exactly as conscious awareness reports a thing, or some event via the five senses. It remains that neither *conscious awareness*, nor *sentient consciousness*, grants *understanding* of that thing or event. Subconscious mind's perceptual faculty, only presents sufficient enough information for the conscious mind to be aware.

Grasp the vital difference. An animals awareness, its perception, and its sentience are necessarily automatic. They must possess (automatic) ability to adapt themselves to nature, exactly because they have no (volitionally conscious) means of changing nature to their purposes.

Although Man possesses the same automatic faculties, *awareness* is where the similarity stops. Instead of *instinctually guiding particular actions*, as happens for animals, Man is only *prompted* by the information given. The automatic process has been intentionally arrested at that point. Creator has determined that conscious awareness, and sentience consciousness, give cause to think. Perception ceases, to engender that Man will use his free will to learn, understand, and then act.

Conscious understanding of these vital distinctions is sadly neglected today. Treating the words *awareness*, *perception*, and *understanding*, as though all mean the same thing, results in Man being inadvertently (or deliberately) given animal status. When volitional consciousness is denied, or overruled, Man's *mental life-blood* is rejected. So he is rendered docile, to be herded like cattle and ruled over by slave masters

Thinking

Man's free will, and the process of thinking, are two different things. Freedom to think means not surrendering the sovereignty of one's mind to anyone, any belief, or anything. Nothing serves one's thought, one's knowledge, or self-mastery, when rulers, neighbours, or imposters are the term-setters of one's mind.

Thinking is choosing to consciously understand existent things, even including theories. Rational thought is the learned process of logic, and reason, so to advance in knowledge and wisdom. Logic is the *art of non-contradictory identification*. Logical reasoning does not rule out one's consideration of feelings, but most emphatically, it rejects feelings, and emotions as tools of identification. Indeed, introspection of feelings may enhance thought and dialogue.

Discernment, is the mental process of discriminatory investigation, so as to reach an understanding. It usefully separates beliefs from truths, illusions from reality, pretences from facts, foolishness from wisdom, and ignorance from knowledge. Intellectual discernment is the key to self-mastery; the tool of rational enquiry based on clarity of thought, and integrity.

Free will

With no cognitive faculty, Man would struggle through life with less than the (automated) perceptual nature of an animal, and no such thing as Man would exist! Without free will, Man cannot function at all! He must choose to activate reason, and silly as it might first seem, unless and until he does, he has no reason to initiate anything. Man has free choice, not only to reason, but to determine what manner of reasoning he will use. (Deductive or Inductive; Subjective or Objective, etc)

Free choice opens or closes the gate to all ideas, truths, postulates, beliefs, wishes, whims, propaganda, and indoctrinations of all kinds. Free will is the gatekeeper of Man's subconscious mind.

Freedom relies on (the chosen process of) reason, whose primary goal is to ascertain what value or life enhancement might result. The greater the value, the higher the will, or intention to achieve or attain it. Free will is the conscious intention to think, and reason, which process will enquire, research, discover, evaluate difficulties, and benefits. Thereafter, one should choose to act responsibly to achieve the desired outcome, or abandon the idea because of its undesirability.

Free will is not a simple yes/no switch. It is the consciously chosen, cognitive process of establishing values and benefits, and rejecting what is not, so as to advance one's life. Free will is self-respect, and self-responsibility in the fullest sense; its reasoned use being life's most critical and important assignment. Data content processed by free will is of our choice, while natural laws of our nature govern the process of how that data is treated. These laws represent your equality with all other living homo sapiens beings.

Creator has facilitated free choice, so that every conceivable nuance of thought is available to every man, woman and child, but none can override the natural laws of our thought processes. Note that severe mind control methods employ torture, and trauma, so as to cancel free will refusal, thus to gain access to the subconscious mind. Less extreme methods may use media, music, entertainment, propaganda, unsubstantiated-beliefs, bogus philosophies, religious persuasions, censorship, and so forth, to open the gate into Man's subconscious mind without his knowing.

Free choice and free will

Will, as a word, may refer to *free will,* or be used as the shortened version of *willpower.* To make this clear, let's separate them.

Free choice is the conscious process of establishing values and benefits that advance one's life, and rejecting what do not. Free will is a commitment to one's free choice. It is an individual's committed responsibility to self; and within that totality, respect for others.

Free will ascertains what values, or life enhancement might result, or are achievable. The greater the value, the higher will be one's committed intention to achieve, or attain it.

That exposes the difference between *free will,* and *willpower.* Free will means to will an action. Will is a conscious, calm, resolved determination, to maintain the mental attitude of intention and commitment, despite any or all temptations to the contrary.

The word *willpower,* joins one's *conscious intention* with subconscious mind's *empowered capacity* to make it happen. In other words, the *will* is of the *conscious* mind, while *power* is subconscious mind's ability to initiate, direct, execute, monitor, and complete one's intention(s). Will is of one's *conscious choice,* while power is exclusively of the *subconscious mind.*

Six higher faculties

Study of our mental faculties should describe those attributes, and distinctions, but alas they do not. All too often, Man's six higher faculties of Perception, Reasoning, Imagination, Intuition, Will, and Memory, are inadequately described in the literature. They are not united in any orderly fashion or sequence. Correlation, interdependency, orderliness and even cooperative effort are absent from present descriptions. Close relationships between conscious mind, subconscious mind, and emotions, are notably absent from all discussion. No communication between them is adequately described. In short, knowledge concerning Man's so-called higher faculties is sadly lacking. Further enquiry seems warranted

It is often said that Man is a *spiritual being* living a *physical life.* What if instead, Man is a spiritual being, living a *spiritual life,* albeit in a physical realm? What if Man is shown to be complete and *spiritual in nature?* Would material resources, products, and material gains, then prove to be tools (or agents) of *spiritual accomplishment,* not merely of materialistic satisfactions, or empire building. That idea will progressively develop over many chapters of this book.

Until now I've discussed Man's cognitive mind, and left his subconscious mind on hold. It's now time to explore its attributes, more importantly, its back and forth communication with conscious mind, because this discourse is Man's spiritual interface with physicality.

4

SUBCONSCIOUS MIND

Patterns of Order

Is it likely that Creator would have provided some control systems that enable our faculties to function in an interdependent, but cooperative manner? Every cell, bone, organ, and system, that is within Mans body, must work within its natural laws or it will fail. Unless corrected, all systems will fail with it. That lesson is of great importance, most especially if applied to society.

Given that chemical factors and a nutritious food supply are the sources of proper bodily functioning, isn't it logical that Mans mental faculties should be fuelled in like manner? Information, or data as it is most commonly called these days, powers our mental faculties. Consciousness is a fuelling process, reliant on our nervous system, and our five senses that interface the external world. Man's brain processes data from his body, and sensory organs, additional to memory as a long-term database, also heart as relating to emotions, feelings and sentient consciousness. Interface of life-process with the external world is the confluence of physicality with spirituality.

Our free will faculty is our conscious mind—our volitional consciousness. Before and after mental processes are automated faculties of the subconscious mind.

- **Conscious Mind:** Volition is firstly free choice to reason and discover, then exercising free will to act on evaluated conclusions.
- **Subconscious Mind:** Perception, imagination intuition, memory, conscience, and emotions are all inclusive. (This sequential order will be more fully understood later in this work.)

Sequential process

Perception is an automated process, as prior discussed. Free will thinking follows, which usually leads to performing an action such as walking, climbing, cooking, or dancing. Walking is not done by the conscious mind instructing left leg muscles, then right, then left, etcetera. Once learned, and memorised, subconscious mind drives the entire (action) process every time walk or dance, for example, is consciously requested.

Grasp the importance of this sequence. Follow the dotted lines in Diagram 5. They show how perception is the automatic starting process. (1) Free will follows. (2) Then automation in the subconscious mind takes over. (3) (Later variations of this diagram will explain more.)

Think about this. We only have two minds, but we have 3 processes that follow one another in sequence. This sequence cannot be reversed. It begins automatically and completes automatically, but who is in charge? Who pulls the strings?

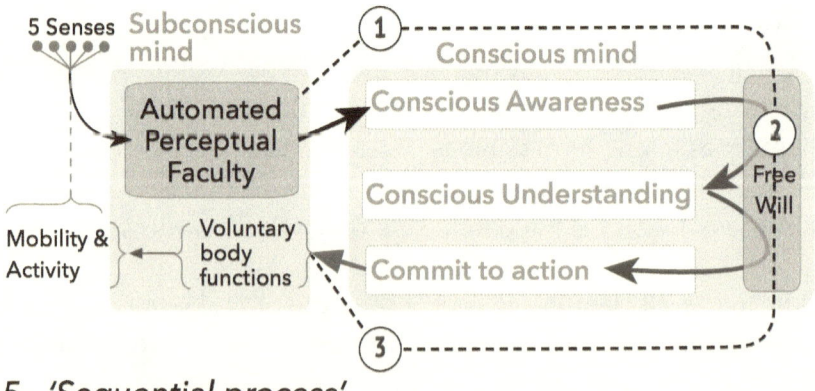

5 - 'Sequential process'

You guessed it, and this revelation is of the most vital importance! The fact that (cognitive) free will is sandwiched between two different processes of our subconscious mind, has far-reaching implications for every aspect of our life. No mention of this sequence is found in literature concerning our six higher faculties, so let's begin that study. Three matters stand out—

1. Man cannot function without exercising free will, else the automated process is starved.
2. The subconscious mind cannot overrule free will; else it is not free.
3. The conscious mind cannot forcibly command subconscious mind; forbidden because the subconscious process is fully automated.

Others implications will soon become apparent. The sheer simplicity of this *sequential process* is almost unbelievable, yet it is entirely real and vitally important. Better yet, no complications exist because automated aspects of the process repeat over and over, round and around for the course of one's life.

This (triple) process is Creator's invitation to every man, woman and child to live a joyous and rewarding life. Natural laws of its processes exist to ensure that you can, if you abide by them, and respect them. Fail, and *just consequences* will take their natural course.

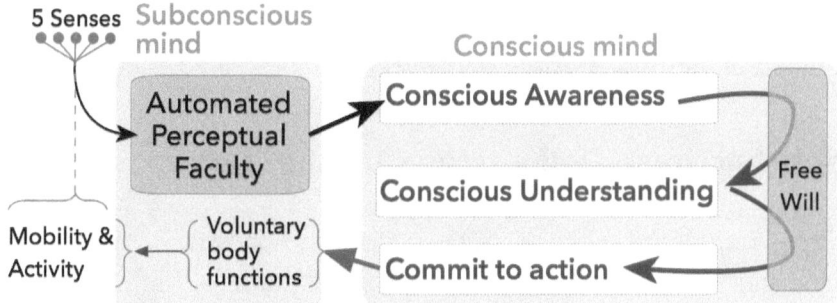

6 - Understanding Sequential process

Man's life is not just an assembly of interactive processes, therefore. Diagram 6 shows that life is a repetitive cycle of mental growth, advancing knowledge, and increasing understanding. Life is as much the feeding of our consciousness with life-enhancing data, as feeding hungry body cells with nutritious foods.

Involuntary functions of the subconscious mind include such as faster breathing, adrenaline release, and reflex actions for example. The diagram conveys the whole mental nature and processes of Mans life in the simplest form, with critical mental processes in their proper sequential order.

Sequence and order did not show up during investigation of Mans six higher faculties. Now they do! It's all so logical. One freely chooses to reason, commits to that goal, and enacts it. Orderly process that surrounds and governs our reasoning faculty and all mental processes is natural law; which upholds our free will 100%

Your subconscious mind takes your every choice, and powers your body through every minute of every day. Although you are not consciously aware of any of it, you are fully in command of it. You can arrest action at any time, just by choosing differently. Each cycle allows for new information via the five senses, while the same process repeats over and over. Each sequence allows new understanding, knowledge, intellectual, and spiritual growth. Mental and body processes are thereby united in service of life. Accordingly, Man is a living, sentient, volitionally conscious being, complete, unified in all respects. Spiritual aspects are described later.

Subconscious – Voluntary vs Involuntary

Triple sequential process, as described and shown, is clearly the vital clue that Mankind has missed for centuries. That's perfectly understandable in many ways, given we've all been brought up on the duality of right versus wrong, or good versus evil; as though two opposing forces. However, once firmly understood that every faculty of Man is tasked by Creator to uphold life, then life itself is the good, and the right. Thereafter, wrong and evil are shown to be deviations from the good, not opposites of equal potency. That idea casts the whole study of mental processes in a new light.

The subconscious mind has two distinct functions, both supportive of life.

First: Involuntary Control: Subconscious mind functions in support of Mans physicality. From the stream of constantly changing information arriving from one's five senses, even while sleeping, it automatically controls all involuntary functions, including heart, lungs, breathing rate, adrenaline release, and so forth, 24/7/365, for decades without sleep. Simultaneously, it monitors and regulates all internal body functions, lungs, heartbeat, blood pH, and so forth. It also produces emotions in the form of feelings; discussed later.

Subconscious mind must necessarily monitor bodily functions, and one's progress, via the five senses, so that muscles and body functions can be adjusted as needed. Intention to succeed, is incontrovertibly bound to every millisecond of one's endeavours, with mind-numbing precision, so as to ensure one's desired success. Witness, for example, the most sensitive and delicate finger movements of a watch repairer, or heart surgeon. Just one (wrong) twitch of a muscle nerve, and his or her most sensitive operation fails. By this example, the subconscious mind is not only bound to administer one's action choices, it is finitely tasked to monitor those activities, nerve by nerve, cell by cell, millisecond by millisecond.

Witness also that in performing a simple task, such as picking up an object and setting it down, one does not have to consciously instruct their body to perform every action in sequence. Instead, subconscious mind does that with flawless precision. It absorbs information from your senses, sees the object, and later feels it. This information processes through the subconscious mind at lightning speed, so that muscle efforts can be instantly and precisely adjusted, as the task progresses, all according to one's freely expressed desires.

Now consider split second (hand and feet) driving complexities, involved in avoiding a potential car accident. Simultaneously, your subconscious mind will direct your eye movements, heart rate, breathing, adrenaline release, and every muscle action required, with split second, mind-numbing precision. It even amasses a few expletives, for emotional release when the car has safely stopped. The vast sum of information, that subconscious mind speedily uses with perfect precision for relatively simple actions, is truly astounding.

One's conscious mind could never handle this data with the same speed, precision, and dexterity. This ability explains why Man has a subconscious mind. It explains the role played by free-will choice in all aspects of adapting his environment to his needs. It also explains why attention must be given to mental health as much as to bodily health.

Second: Voluntary Control: Subconscious mind accepts one's free-will instructions to act, (e.g., talk, listen, climb, eat, drive, dance, etc.) It then controls all necessary muscle functions in honour of free choice. There is a strong parallel, between absorbing and processing mental data, and the ingestion and processing of food.

It is clear that Creator has employed the principles of Mans bodily functioning, for his mental control processes. In other words, natural laws that govern Mans functioning, exist in the biological, conscious, and subconscious planes. Should we have expected anything other? Do they also exist in the emotional, and/or spiritual planes?

As prior explained, automated processing of data ceases, after the subconscious mind has delivered material evidence to one's conscious mind, thereby prompting it to deal with that information. Once a evaluative decision is reached, and one commits to an action, subconscious mind resumes automatic functioning, which, of course, means that free will has finished work, for the present.

Parameters of subconscious mind

Whereas *orderliness* had not shown previously, now natural law very eminently shows in Mans higher faculties.

Boundaries are evident.

- The subconscious mind is open to conscious sway, but never to external influence, save that permitted by free will.
- If the subconscious mind were not open to change, by one's conscious mind, one's free will would be ineffective, or insufficient.
- If the subconscious mind were open to unchecked outside influence, its functionality would be raided, robbed, or violated.
- The subconscious mind cannot discern, evaluate, adjudicate, judge, or create. To do so would overrule free will choices, and undermine cognitive abilities.
- Obversely, subconscious mind's automated processes cannot be overridden, or countermanded by the conscious mind.
- Accordingly, the subconscious mind refuses all (mental) harm, save that which free will admits.

Human consciousness can be considered to have five separate abilities—

1. Conscious mind: Volitional conscious. (Cognitive ability and free will.)
2. Subconscious perception and integration, that together feed sentient, and conscious awareness.
3. Subconscious control of body functions, and motor actions. (Muscular control)
4. Subconscious monitoring of all the above, that when integrated with freely chosen value choices, conscience and emotions result.

5. Subconscious assimilation of one's chosen values, choices, and actions, as one's *soul*.

When the 6 higher faculties are included, all neatly fit inside the sequential process—

1. **Subconscious Mind**: Perception, Imagination, Intuition
2. **Conscious Mind**: Volition, first being free choice, then reasoning, then free will determination. Also, life-value assessments, yet to be described.
3. **Subconscious Mind**: Motor skills and body monitoring, Memory, Conscience, Emotions

The above parameters present cautions. For example, Mans wilful refusal to engage *conscious understanding* forces him to function in a state akin to animality—to depend entirely on his automated processes. It cannot be done because he is not so equipped! Man advances if he chooses, but tragically, remains bound to a state of (perceptual) *conscious awareness*, akin to a state of animality, if he refuses to properly use his cognitive faculties.

Because free will is sandwiched between two fully automated subconscious processes, no directives from alternate, or additional sources, divine, or otherwise, can take effect without free will acceptance. Each man and woman *is the (conscious) arbiter of what he or she admits, or refuses.*

That is what free will means. It is freedom to think and act, unaffected by anything save what conscious mind agrees or accepts.

> *'It is the mark of an educated mind to be able to entertain a thought without accepting it.'—Aristotle*

Your life is yours.

5

INTELLECTUAL TOOLS AND FACULTIES

Knowledge and consciousness

1. **Knowledge** is acquaintance with facts, truths, or principles—one's understanding from study or investigation. The intellect's capacity to retain knowledge is called intellectual memory. One chooses to learn, but memory is automatic.
2. **Full consciousness** means consciously and consistently using the integrated sum of one's knowledge, previously acquired.

Fullness does not imply a finite measure. It means choosing to apply one's present understanding, irrespective of one's level of education. A young child, and a wise old sage, can both use the fullness of whatever understanding each possesses. Full consciousness is not the raising of it, the increasing of it, or some new vibration of it. It just means not cheating yourself, not being apathetic, not dodging what might seem onerous. It is one's full intellectual diligence, fortitude, and integrity, all in one parcel.

Its opposite polarity is mental abandonment, exactly what that term means; desertion, neglect, betrayal of one's true self.

Integration

Concepts beautifully explain the process of integration, which facilitates the 'sequential process'.

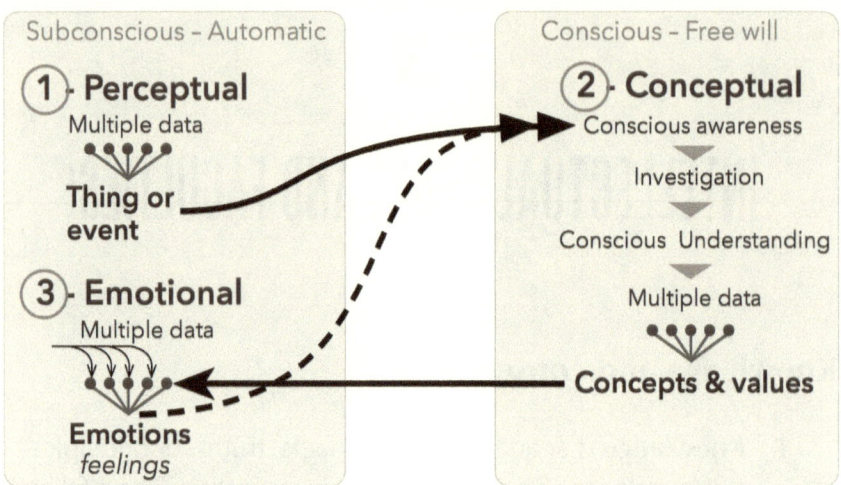

7 - Sequential Integration

1. **Perceptual integration**: The first automatic co-faculty of the subconscious mind.
2. **Conceptual integration**: (sandwiched by 1 and 3) Facilitation and inducement to consciously use free will. To integrate, formulate concepts, and principles. To use reason, and logic, in concert with the laws of identity, and causality. To gain and to use knowledge, for the advancement and furtherance of one's life and ambitions.
3. **Emotional integration:** The automatic faculty that is subconscious mind, plus involuntary control and functioning.

The first, and third of these integrating processes, use images for integrating data. (A picture contains a thousand words.) The cognitive mind uses word concepts. All have an orderly process, and since order means law in etymology, natural law is evident within Mans mental, emotional, and physical life-processes, including *the triple sequential process*.

Let's now consider some of Mans other mental faculties. What follows, will in some cases be different from that commonly taught, for reasons already given.

Whereas the vocabulary of the conscious mind is *word concepts*, the subconscious mind uses an *image vocabulary*. This difference means that each time data passes from the conscious mind to subconscious mind, and vice versa, it must be transmitted by vocabulary amenable to the recipient, or it will not register.

Concepts

Conscious understanding almost invariably rests upon comprehending a multiplicity of data, that Mans mind does not have ready ability to process. Data needs to be condensed into a useable size to facilitate cognitive processing. Concepts serve this purpose perfectly.

They integrate information. Concepts carry vast amounts of information in one or two words. Conceptualising, allows for the mental processing of large quantities of data with least mental effort. Each new word concept serves a particular purpose in advancing one's knowledge. Concepts are named to become words. Language and communication derive from this ability. Without language, we cannot think or reason. Aside from proper names, all words are concepts, e.g., book, wallet, bicycle, vegetable.

Concepts offer the use of logic, and reason. They allow Man to consider alternatives rapidly, to evaluate, judge, and decide upon actions in an instant. They enable one to remember meanings, judgements, and conclusions. They facilitate quick recall of past understandings, and thus are the core attribute of intuition.

In sum, concepts are a representational abstraction, gleaned from existent reality, and thus anchored to it. They are neither concretes, nor fictions. Concepts provide a method of mentally grasping and dealing with identifiable complexities that exist. They have no content or meaning apart from their (real) constituent units.

The process of concept-formation involves the integrating of events and observations into a tight context, by grasping relationships, differences, and similarities. Conceptualising is the process of drawing inferences, of making deductions, of reaching conclusions, of asking new questions, and of discovering new answers, expanding one's knowledge into an ever-growing sum.

By organising perceptual material into concepts, thence into wider and still wider concepts, Man can grasp, retain, identify, and integrate vast amounts of knowledge, extending far beyond the immediate concretes of any given moment.

Intuition

Intuit awareness is the conscious reminding of something that was previously learned. The phrase, *I knew it intuitively*, is fundamentally accurate, but let's be cautious. Intuit information may indeed be the direct remembrance of truth. Equally, it may not. It may, instead, be the direct recollection of beliefs, propaganda, or indoctrinations, having little or no truthful foundation.

Potential to mislead begs knowing whether past information was prior-investigated, evaluated, or authenticated. It may result from beliefs, assertions, indoctrinations, bogus philosophies, media, or educational propaganda. Most certainly, intuition is not some divine inspiration, 6th sense awakening, spiritual manifestation, angelic invocation, energy prompting, or mystical revelation.

Or is it? If such-like are what some folk hold to be true, then their intuitions will be founded on what they've accepted as truthful, whether that be, or not. If one's knowledge is factually based, and objective, then intuition profitably advances one's life. Fictions regurgitated as truths, will not.

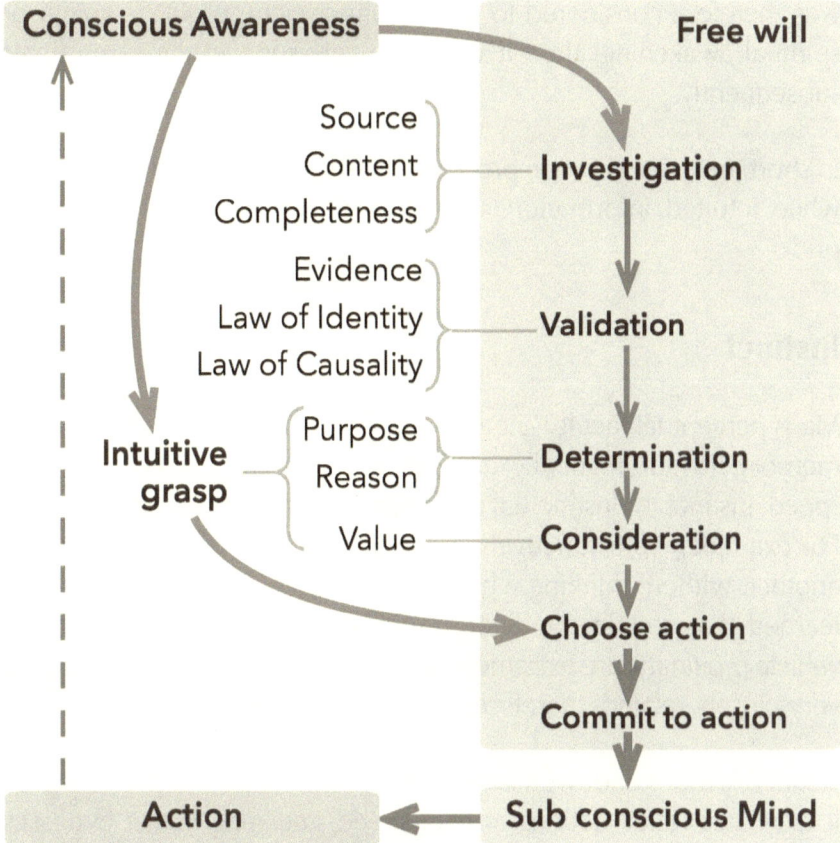

8 – Investigative and Intuitive Processes

Right and left pathways in diagram 8 function in tandem, according to one's choices. Information not intuited, should properly be investigated (Right side), while information that has been validated, or even assimilated without validation, will present intuitively. (Left side)

As shown in the diagram, intuitive information will automatically include some degree of purpose, reason, and value, because of past thoughts and actions that trigger it. The extent to which intuited information is valuable, will depend on one's previous determination; past enquiry and acceptance, as the right-hand side of the diagram illustrates. If the investigation had prior confirmed truthfulness, and was therefore considered to offer advancement, profit, learning, or spiritual awakening, then it will intuitively support the same goals subsequently.

In short, fresh information prompts investigation, and authentication, while intuited information should properly have been examined prior.

Instinct

Mans perceptual faculty accepts data from the five senses, and from memory, to automatically activate life-preserving actions at light speed. Instinct, or instinctual action thus described, is a reflex action. For example, we instinctively brake to avoid our car slamming into another, without thinking whether we should or not. We've already learned that certain conditions, such as closing speed, and close vehicle proximity, are extremely dangerous. Instinct, and intuition are very closely related, therefore, but with one huge difference.

Instinct, is Mans endowed faculty of self-protection and preservation. It facilitates reflex actions at light-speed, meaning that it bypasses all conscious thought processes that ordinarily take time. Man's instinctive, or reflex action, is thereby limited to (immediate) impending danger; vital for self-preservation. Pausing to consider is far too dangerous, when potential disaster is imminent.

It follows that *life preserving immediacy* is reflex action. Whereas intuit information prompts further consideration, *instinctive action* is fully automated. All else reserves for free will investigation, and free choice.

Study diagram 9, and you'll see that instinctive actions bypass free will. Intuitive data does not, but it does circumvent conscious deliberation. Thus it may deliver untruths, fallacies and false beliefs.

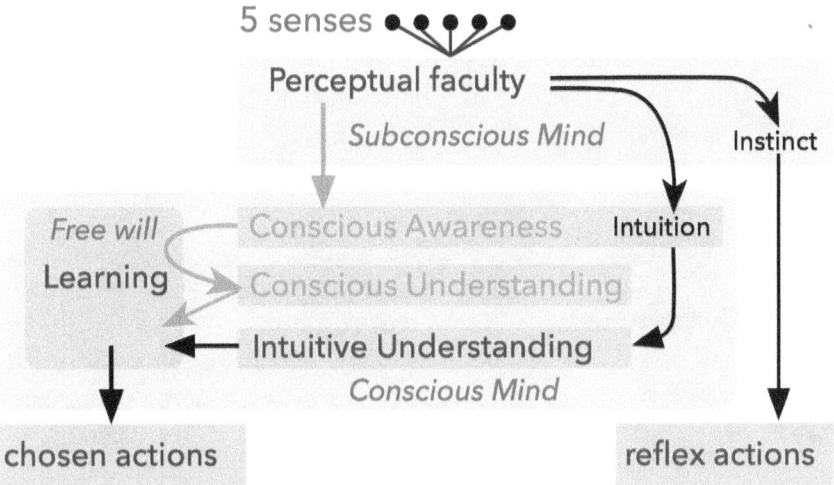

9 - Intuitive and Instinctive Processes

Beliefs

A proper understanding of intuition, inexorably leads to the subject of beliefs versus knowledge. Properly understood, beliefs are mental propositions, or proposals held in abeyance while they pass through examination, from possibilities, through probabilities, to certain knowledge.

As a containment, or holding tool, therefore, a belief is neither true, nor false. Uncertainty implies that information should pass through a sequential process of validation. If shown to be true, or false, it becomes knowledge, whereby *belief* cancels. For example—

- I am consciously aware of something that may be true, or false.
- I believe its truth may benefit me. (I will seek further.)
- I believe it likely to be true. (But many doubts remain.)
- I believe that its truth is highly probable. (More evidence please.)
- Now I know it to be true, or false. (I have no further need to believe.)

- I will hold this evidence as knowledge of truth, or falsity, until, or unless some new evidence controverts it.
- I will live according to what I know to be true.
- I am grateful for the (conceptual) tool of *belief* that assisted my learning.

Validation	Axiomatic
	Knowledge – Proven Knowledge
Completeness	High certainty
	Very strong probability – Certainty
Evidence	Strong evidence – Confirmations
	Possibilty – Likely – Very likely
Investigation	Supportive data
Law of Identity & Causality	Asertions – Beliefs
	Propaganda – Rumours – Whims
Content	Mind control – Indoctrinations

10 – Investigation and Validation

Beliefs are like shopping baskets that hold items through to checkout, whereby, the basket remains in the store for the next customer. Truths, being your purchases, or fruits of investigation, are factual knowledge you take home.

Sadly the word *belief* has become so elastically pliable today, that one cannot know whether it delivers truth, or not. The word has become a mental excuse, allowing one to say what they consider to be true, while artfully avoiding any charge of being certain. Worse, it seems, we are expected to apologise for being certain, in case someone's feelings are offended. Belief systems (theoretically) relieve any need to exercise diligent conscious enquiry, whereby the whole sham self-perpetuates. Certainty is held to be intolerance of another's beliefs, in many cases.

Imagination

Among Mans 6 higher faculties, imagination is often described as the faculty, or action of forming new ideas, or images, of external objects not present to the senses. Further, imagination imparts clarity to thoughts, or to ideas being formed, enabling clear expression of an idea to self, or others. Likewise, it assists in accomplishing a particular goal, or objective, by holding the image of its completion in view. The easiest way to grasp the idea is to visualise it as complete, to see it in your mind's eye, as vividly as if it already existed.

All the above is true, but Man's ability to form mental pictures in his mind, is vastly more important than those descriptions convey. Subconscious mind's vocabulary is images, that the faculty of imagination excels in doing. Thus imagination is a method of transferring data from the word vocabulary of the conscious mind, to the different vocabulary of the subconscious mind. Perception facilitates the reverse order.

Free will is the access pathway to both. It facilitates the delivery of images to the subconscious mind, and conversely, it investigates that which it becomes consciously, or sentiently aware of.

Altogether, this testifies how information traverses, between the conscious mind and subconscious mind, in two-way conversations. Now, the reason for sandwiching (conscious) free will, between two processes of Man's subconscious mind, becomes vibrantly clear. Creator did not miss one thing.

Memory

Memory is sometimes attributed to some infinite, eternal mind, seemingly because neuroscience seems unable to find where it nests in the human body. Why do we invent such notions?

Given that concepts such as velocity, ratios, leverage, rotation, inertia, and sequence, inherently make an engine work as a function of design, but are not tangible, or material things, so memory is an internal function of the subconscious process, and is not physical.

Memory is present moment conscious awareness of learned information; one's conscious recollection of subconsciously stored data. Memory is the subconscious process of storing and recalling. As prior discussed, memory fuels our intuit and instinct faculties. Equally as discussed for intuition, memorised information may not be truthful, insofar as it supports and upholds one's life.

Sequential process, here described, heralds a vibrant new understanding of our mental processes, especially concerning Mans six higher faculties. It offers new enlightenment for the our species, never previously described. Whereas orderliness or natural laws are seldom found in the literature, now they abound.

Once cannot help but see the parallel of this enlightenment in societal terms. Every living man and woman is unique, yet we are all equal in natural law process. Thus a blueprint for society lies within each of us. Our task is to discover it, learn from it, and employ it. The next few chapters open that doorway. The more one travels this pathway, the simpler it becomes.

6

LIFE-VALUES

The constant alternative of life or death necessitates that we act according to our nature. Since life is of supreme importance, it becomes necessary to define, and pursue what will sustain and uphold it. Values outside of life, are nonsense. If one chooses only to exist then no real values are possible, no code of ethics makes sense, and no moral actions are necessary. So we should determine what values life requires, and pursue those goals.

> It is only the concept of 'Life' that makes the concept of 'Value' possible. —Ayn Rand

Man chooses what to eat, what to drink, and what air quality to breathe. None of those choices affects how his cardio-vascular system works, or how his immune, respiratory, circulatory, or skeletal systems work. Nonetheless, every atom in Mans body depends on the value of what he eats, drinks, and inhales. The same applies to the (value) quality of thought, including the validity of all information, beliefs, superstitions, and ideologies.

Creator has determined that your subconscious mind remains fully focussed on upholding your life. Everything else is secondary. Therefore, subconscious mind seeks to know if your conscious mind is on the same page; whether your free will endorses the *value of life* that it is tasked to uphold. It desires to harmonise with you, to cooperate, to live life to its fullest, and most joyous. So it invites your full conscious support.

Subconscious mind, asks you to inform what *value* you place on your actions. It cannot monitor your efforts, nor report progress by way of feelings, unless it knows what you consider to be *value*.

Values are a choice

Only you can provide this life-value information. We each can choose what to value, and how much. We can decide not to value. However, subconscious mind cannot function in a mental vacuum, any more than a stomach can process food when starved.

Life-values are perhaps best described, as a particular value that you trust a certain task will bring to your life. Truth, honesty, integrity, graciousness, diligence, or perseverance are virtues, more so than examples of life-values. Nonetheless, *virtues* attach to a *material value* most often, e.g., I will study diligently. Knowledge, for this example, is a material gain, while diligence expresses one's willingness to ensure that it is pertinent, useful, and supportive of life. Accordingly, the term *life-values,* best describes *what will add valued meaning or spiritual quality to your life experience*, over and *above any material gain.*

It is from *life-sustaining* concepts, that a personal *code of ethics* may develop. Such reference base will contribute to life's sustenance, and ever growing achievements, in any chosen field of endeavour. Once selected, and impressed on the subconscious mind, life-values fuel your emotional database, in satisfaction of healthy and rewarding reports, that we call feelings.

Values – Material versus spiritual

A burglar places a high value on freedom of choice, tax avoidance, not having to be employed, and so forth. He substitutes the plunder of value, that he regards as smart achievement, in place of creating, or producing 'life-values.' He deceives himself, by substituting material value for spiritual value.

Real values, that underpin his activities, and about which he knows nothing, are his desire to escape from the nature of his being, to escape from natural laws that impel productive effort in satisfaction of his life. He seeks a mental cop-out, deriving emotional satisfaction from looting material values, in place of creating spiritual values. (Taxation is of the same ilk.) A burglar must use his mind nevertheless. Success entirely depends on it. He prepares every move with mental precision, without which failure is inevitable.

Burglars, and all those who thrive on value-theft, have no idea they are nothing but cannibal-minded second-handers. They've no understanding of their reliance and dependence on every life-value created by others. Material values are their only concern, which they plunder for emotional satisfactions with great joy.

Tragically, others do recognise this evil and thrive on exploiting it. Criminals, aka corporate governments, write voluminous tax codes to protect their corrupt thieving. The undeniable truth is that every wicked, criminal victimisation in history, rests on the premise of stolen (material) values. This includes government taxes! You produce; we rob!

Values - Importance

Life-values imply that we reason, not just what we wish to accomplish, or gain, but also why. We may think, consider, evaluate, and judge what real values we want in life, e.g. new wardrobe, or vacation, but why we want these things casts their choice in a different light. What virtue or spiritual satisfaction will result? Why, exactly, is a particular material gain valuable?

The importance of life-values is inestimable; greater than anything taught in religion, philosophy, psychology, or any sciences of Man, I submit. Today's world is awash with articles describing how we should raise our vibrations, or our consciousness. How many of these folk advise, that without choosing values, pertinent to life itself, that our conscious and subconscious processes are mentally and spiritually starved?

We're all taught that we cannot control our subconscious mind, and this is true. So most folks are stopped in their tracks. Instead, we should learn that we *cannot control its process*, but we *can indeed influence its value content*, its reference base. We can alter the *values* it works with, by deliberately and assertively taking conscious care of our life, mentally, just as nutritious food aids bodily health. It should now be clear that *life-values* are the tool for influencing or programming our subconscious mind.

Values constitute the program, that is your subconscious mind. What you freely *choose to value,* will *source your emotions,* meaning that you are consciously in charge of your life. Your subconscious mind will support your choices, without fail. Fail yourself, however, abandon values, and it will support that choice; whether you like it or not.

Values - Default

Please be cautioned. Any *life-value*, whether consciously assigned, or automatically assimilated by the subconscious mind, once accepted, will remain firm until replaced, by another that overrides its importance. In short, *past values remain until substituted*, despite their length of stay.

Here lies potential disaster. False values almost invariably lead to life-harming actions and practices, including mental traumas. Every lie, unverified acceptance, false belief, erroneous ideology, or soul-destructive theology, may easily, indeed very likely, will be accepted as one's values, unless asserted to the contrary. Emotional consequences, erroneously known as negative emotions, will result in corresponding measure.

Notice that a concert pianist, corrupt lawyer, wise elder, burglar, acclaimed physician or rapist, have all their chosen their own value set. Some advance life, while others are contrarily evil. Nonetheless, each receives emotional encouragement from their successes, regardless of their contribution to the human species, or their detraction from it. Subconscious mind, *accepts for value,* what each consciously *nominates is their value.* Subconscious mind cannot overrule their choice.

If, for any action, you do not allocate a life-value, the subconscious mind will fill the vacuum with your nearest value, e.g., one chosen last week, from your previous marriage, your last job, or in your childhood. You may never realise that you ever picked such a value, or disvalue in your past, but your subconscious mind remembers, because that's one of its primary tasks.

Thus life-values are chosen by you, knowingly, or unknowingly. Some will complain bitterly, e.g., *'you mean I've got to mentally ascribe a life-value for every damn thing I do, every second of the day; you're kidding I hope!'* No, I'm not joking, and no, life-values can be made sublimely simple, so much so that they may only need revision once every month, three, or six. The reason is that *life-values are more an enduring attitude,* an underlying, yet addressable subconscious program, based on the need to act to sustain one's life—*from a spiritual perspective.* Do you have to upgrade your computer software each minute, or day? No, but it does need to be updated periodically.

Actions contrary to those that sustain life, will drain one's time, energy, motivation, and resources. It follows in all logic that any surrender of *life's value,* for the sake of a lesser one, represents the sacrifice of one's life; little by little without ever knowing. If one does not choose to value his or her life, and thus fully live, nature will take its course based on that choice. Who would want to leave their life to random chance?

Value Based Living

The more personal, and value-charged one's thinking is, the clearer, truer, and more it enriches one's life. A science of ethics and morality, based on the science and nature of Man, is not only achievable, but is written within our very nature, yet this fact is least well known. We understand that contaminated food is poison, and that contaminated ideas are mental poison. Accordingly, a science of ethics and morality needs do little more than distinguish mental and spiritual food from contaminating ideas, in personal, and societal terms. How much simpler can it be?

If we base each new endeavour or task, on rationally chosen *life-enhancing values*, then that ethic is automatically impressed on our subconscious mind. It will echo in our feelings. Rational ethics may, therefore, be described as consistently practising one's chosen life-values.

Then we've a self-reinforcing two-way street. Having impressed life-supporting values in our subconscious mind, so it returns the favour. Conscience reminds our cognitive mind, of previously chosen values concerning any newly proposed actions. Subconscious mind informs, or reinforces our value choices, through conscience and emotions.

Values are Vital

Values corresponding with life enhancement should properly be called spiritual values. Can these be changed periodically? Can adult values replace teenage values, for example? Certainly, but they are more difficult to alter, than to first assign them.

- You cannot change your mind; you can only change its content.
- You cannot change your emotional responses, but you can revise the values from which feelings automatically generate.
- Altogether you cannot change your life without mastering your values, by first taking charge of your consciousness.

An article, entitled *A Unified Theory of Ethics*, states—

> There will be no shake-up (let alone revolution) in ethics unless emotion drives the reasoning, just as well as vice versa. [*Notice how (one's) two minds mutually respect each other in that sentence.*]
>
> [But] beliefs can be specified and managed whereas we can't define, explain, nor predict emotions: we can propositions; but we know next to nothing about emotions. *No psychologist of which I am aware has a comprehensive theory of emotions which I find emotionally-satisfying* (i.e. persuasive to me.)
>
> I propose that *adding value be the one norm, or operating principle that we need* to have to incentivize and to motivate us in the ethical direction. —Marvin C. Katz, Ph.D.[7] [Emphasis mine]

Katz gets it fully! Neither had I seen emotions explained in a manner that satisfied their purpose, or import. The reason is clear. Little in literature concerning emotions, speaks of life-values and our ability to programme our subconscious mind. Where are life-values taught as life's fundamentals in psychology, psychotherapy, philosophy, or any other human science? The field is vacant.

Life is Mans supreme value. Its value should found all life sciences, and the humanities.

Katz continues—

How does one achieve this added value? One must be aware of him/herself and be detached from the negative thoughts, impulses, and negative conditioning from external sources. Therefore, one needs to know how to work on him/herself. Maybe the next step is to put together some ways in which people can practice working on their being—.—Marvin C. Katz, Ph.D.[7]

Working on oneself, so as to add value, is what I'll describe later as the means to master emotions, and to live a joyous, emotional, and spiritual life. Man is gifted far and beyond most folks understanding. Our personal values, and desire to exercise them, define our true (spiritual) self, but as Katz offers, one needs to know how to work on him/herself.

A method for programming the subconscious mind is the next chapter.

Values – Infants

Infant children, offer the best example for studying how the subconscious mind may be programmed. Their ability is remarkable given that infants cannot speak, they have no innate ideas, no science, no math, and no language. Here's how infants program their subconscious minds, absent those abilities.

Exactly as Mans automatic perceptual faculty allows one to become consciously aware of a thing, place, or event, so for an infant who cannot yet crawl, his or her conscious mind acknowledges, or sees a place beyond reach. His or her conscious mind curiously asks, what is it? To satisfy this curiosity, the infant desires to explore, which means it must get from where it presently is, to *there*. (Watch how infant children will stretch out an arm and wriggle their fingers almost as though pointing.)

A conscious choice to explore, is the infant's request to the subconscious mind, to get me *there*. The subconscious mind responds, in honour and respect for this desire. It begins activating muscles to satisfy the infant's request. It assimilates, and integrates all the data involved in accomplishing this goal. This information includes the intention, envisaged value, or benefit, what muscles are involved, what body adjustments are necessary and need monitoring, and what constitutes success or failure. Despite this may take several attempts, free will pleads with the subconscious mind to continue— all the while, the infant knows absolutely nothing about this process.

Understand what is happening. An infant's subconscious perception consists of images, no different from that of an adult. Looking at some place, wishing to explore, presents that (different place) image to subconscious mind, as his or her desire to be *there*. Just looking intently at this intended destination is sufficient, because the language of the subconscious mind is images. If the mission succeeds, a feeling of joy will result. If not, the infant feels disappointment, or failure of a kind, but has no words to describe it. So it cries. Given reasonable health, and opportunity, the infant will ultimately succeed, however.

Please grasp the vital importance of this monumental achievement. This babe in the woods, this tender infant, has taught its subconscious mind one of the most valuable lessons in life, without words, without concepts, without any conscious understanding, without any mentoring, or outside influence whatsoever. The infant becomes consciously aware of a place, automatically. It has exercised its conscious free will. It has willed to be *there*, thus giving subconscious mind a (valued) life reason to get me *there*—to explore, investigate, see, touch, feel, taste—so to advance my life. Although the infant is in conscious control of his/her mind and body, he/she does not understand how any of his/her conscious processes work. Desire is wanting to be *there*, not an instruction to get me *there*.

Subconscious mind must integrate the idea of *there*, with the necessary muscle actions of getting *there*. It complies in full because it is tasked to support and advance life. The motions of crawling become learned, wherein the subconscious mind monitors every nerve and cell in the body, observes progress through the five senses, compares these with the (expressed) value of being *there*, and reports a feeling of joy, or sorrow, according to success, or failure.

Values – Allowance

This whole process is so simple, and so logical, when viewed sequentially. It just flows. That's how simple and uncomplicated an intentioned life and learning should be.

Creator's method works to perfection. It cannot be otherwise, because no conscious knowledge, no extraneous diversions, or any perversion of truth such as propaganda, or false ideologies, can interfere. Two factors are important—

- The infant's mind is *tabula-rasa*, meaning it is a blank slate with no innate ideas, or mental content.
- Perception is automatic access to raw data concerning the material world; unpolluted save by conscious mind; which faculty the infant still has not learned to use.

As prior mentioned, the cognitive process uses the vocabulary of (word) concepts, but as yet, the infant has no words. Direct image communication to the subconscious mind must take place, else nothing accomplishes.

Because the infant's cognitive mind is blank, fundamentally disabled, conscious understanding must be by-passed, as diagram 11 shows. Until the rudiments of learning, and thinking have begun, the conscious mind can offer nothing. Consequently, the perceptual faculty must bridge, through free will to committed actions, as the fat (curved) arrow shows.

This understanding is profound beyond all measure, a fundamental truth that science is only now beginning to grasp. Perception has interfaced directly via free choice, with subconscious control and monitoring, completely bypassing the (cognitive) conscious process. Diagram 11 shows however that all other faculties work as for adults.

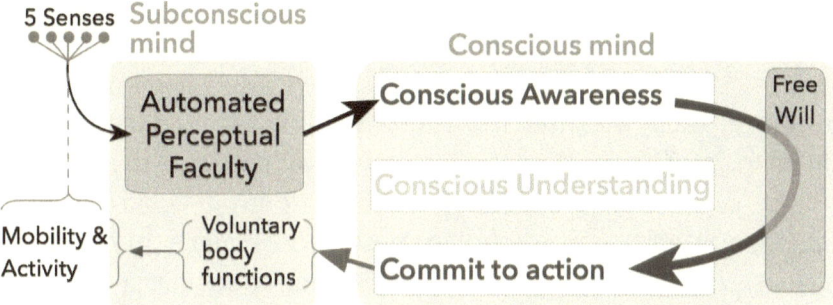

11 - By-pass Understanding

Although cognitive understanding is by-passed, free will is still honoured. Infants, and young children are enabled to choose their actions, and to experience the emotions of success or failure, while they steadily grow in cognitive mental stature, thereby adding to their database of understanding. Ethics, and virtues, progressively implant into the subconscious mind of an infant, once basic words such as yes, and no, are grasped.

This process fosters learning, and ability to develop an understanding over time, to grow, to advance and to live honestly. It serves to instruct Man about subconscious mind programming, and how he can consciously implant values into his subconscious mind. Its purpose is Man's material advancement and spiritual accomplishment, nothing less. As an experiential window, it allows for an infant's conscious development, over time, according to his or her ability and mental focus.

As a lesson in free will expression, opportunity to progress at one's own pace is perhaps the most beautiful natural law, ever bestowed by Creator. It is Creator's *Natural Law of Allowance*. This law not only allows infants to grasp understanding in the fullest context, but it also allows adults to mature at their pace, equally applicable to those who are mentally handicapped. It truly is a beautiful thing.

Values allowance for Infants

Suppose later, that the (now crawling) infant understood the mechanics of conscious and subconscious process. Imagine that tiny he, or she, had a vocabulary, and consciously grasped that one's intention to act triggered certain muscle movements, to effect the desired result. Suppose also that the infant knew that a *life-value* offers a passionately valued reason to subconscious mind. Perhaps then, for learning to walk, this tiny tot might address his/her subconscious mind in this manner—

> 'Hey subconscious, that crawling thing we did, was totally awesome. Now I want you to learn about walking upright using the same process, same standards, same deal. It seems I need you to manage my leg muscles for decades. I'm really passionate about getting upright on my two legs instead of dragging my backside along the floor, so please help me stand upright, and be mobile. Don't miss a single step buddy, excuse the pun, or I'll be back on my bum!'

Silly as it may seem, a dialogue of that kind is the most beneficial things that a kid, or adult can do. The practice of directly addressing one's subconscious mind, even vocally, perhaps instead of singing under the shower, is a life skill seldom if ever taught. It is extremely beneficial and powerful beyond measure! It is the core platform of the three step—one minute program, described later.

I've shown how an infant can succeed with no cognitive understanding, no concepts and no word vocabulary. Can cognitive knowledge be by-passed, thefore? Are excuses permitted? No!

> Man is born with an emotional mechanism, just as he is born with a cognitive mechanism; but, at birth, both are tabula rasa. [a blank slate] It is man's cognitive faculty, his mind, that determines the content of both. —Ayn Rand

Please read that quotation carefully. Man's mind determines the content of his cognitive abilities *and his emotions*. Let's explore this further.

Given all five senses function in normal health, emotions begin as soon as externalities are available to an infant's senses. Primary emotions trigger when they act, or are acted upon, e.g., when they are fed, comforted, or sleep deprived. Almost identical to physically felt pleasure, or pain, joy or sorrow best explain an infant's primary emotions. These testify that subconscious mind is monitoring, and reporting life's progress, or non-progress. Nothing could be more simple, or elementary.

Values allowance for Adults

Maturity comes from grown mental ability to supplant the *Law of Allowance*, progressively accepting full adult cognitive responsibility; consciously enquiring, discerning, evaluating, and understanding truth, so as to exercise value-based choices. Adolescence is that platform of maturity.

Perception is the trigger that prompts thought, not muscle activity as for animals, neither mere muscle activity for infants. By adolescence, cognitive understanding, and responsible decision making, should have become common everyday practice. A reliable store of knowledge, and full conscious ability, should properly have replaced all reliance on Creator's *natural Law of Allowance*.

> When I was a child, I spake as a child, I understood as a child, I thought as a child: but when I became a man, I put away childish things. —King James Bible. 1 Corinthians 13:11[iv]

Nevertheless, the *Law of Allowance* does not fully cancel. Creator has allowed that it remain, for learning, and mental maturity, to grow and become habituated through choice, according to one's abilities, throughout one's entire adult life. Habituation of this process at one's pace, enables consistently high percentiles of truth to amass in one's intuit database, in turn fostering greater reliability, and certainty, with least effort.

Do you see Creator's graciousness—the purposeful tool by which slow learners, and those who are mentally restricted, can best participate among not so handicapped equals? Do you see Creator's fervent desire that you be all that you choose to be, at your pace? It is not compassion. It is Creator's facilitation of ever increasing mental efficiency, over time. Mental, and emotional development, is clearly an incumbent responsibility, for a full and prosperous life.

Values-- Subliminal programming

Although discoveries, and actions of young children yield different emotions, and though some disappoint, their life is predominantly one of excitement, and revelations. Each hour, or day, is an exciting new vision of reality, of life, and of vibrant new possibilities.

Hold that thought. Babysitter television offers new images also. These can program the subconscious mind of very young children—even intentionally. Do you see the potential problem? Young children, have not yet developed their full cognitive abilities. They're still dependent on the *Law of Allowance,* to some appreciable degree. They're still reliant, in part, on images as their source of understanding. So their emotions will reflect what they see.

Now consider the difference. Out in the woods, or playground, actions of young children also yield emotions, but these are pertinently instructive. Children's life in the outdoors is real. What actions they choose, and why, result in feelings that inform of their choices. So they learn the cause of failures, and successes, and the value of rational deliberation beforehand.

Babysitter television offers nothing of the kind. It rivets the child's attention, demanding subjective concentration. It switches their mind from exciting experiences, and discoveries, to passive absorption. Producers know that reasons, and explanations, will kill rapt attention, so they focus on excitement and drama, and counterposed emotions. Of crucial importance, here, is that emotions do not spontaneously originate, as in a playground. So the child is deprived of first-hand learning, and exposed to passive indoctrination.

Because the child is still growing cognitively, and is still influenced to a degree by perceptual imagery, via the *Law of Allowance,* so TV images will very likely impact the child's subconscious mind. Indeed this may be the express intention of a producer. Values may be subconsciously implanted, without the child, or parents, consciously knowing. Adults may be similarly influenced, by what we affectionately call soapies and sitcoms. Subliminal advertising may further add deleterious effects. Technical trickery can implant images that bypass conscious recognition. While free will accepts the program's totality as relevant, so the trick image is granted immediate subconscious acceptance.

All of this extracts a devastating toll on humankind. Authority, instruction, statute laws, mental diversion, religious indoctrination, babysitter TV, censorship, and much more, not forgetting parental edicts, e.g. *'you must learn to conform,'* are sufficient to suffocate full conscious development. After that, authority, religious dogma, subjectivism, mysticism, misguiding philosophy, even culture, and customs exact a devastating toll on mankind.

> Give me the child until he is seven and I'll give you the man
> —St. Francis Xavier (1506-1552)

Indeed! Nothing underscores trespass of the *Law of Allowance* better than that quotation from 500 years ago. St. Francis fully understood how a child's mind is influenced at an early age, especially when nourished with regular doses of dogma. The child would grow into a man or woman, unable to rid themselves of noxious beliefs, or debilitating theories planted in their innocent, unsuspecting, unquestioning, subconscious minds—never overcome.

It's not religion merely. Secular philosophy still clings to Emmanuel Kant, Rene Descartes, Sigmund Freud, and many disciples who extol the same principles. Keynesian economic theory, that today props up fiat money systems, and fraudulent banking practices, also relies on theories planted in unquestioning, subconscious minds—never to be overcome.

Values – Abuse of allowance

Woe betides those who abuse Creators Law of Allowance!

> You can ignore reality, but you can't ignore the consequences of ignoring reality. —Ayn Rand.

The *Law of Allowance* exists to offer lessons of support and correction—usually through feelings—its lessons to be consciously woven into the tapestry of one's conscious, and subconscious minds.

The *Law of Allowance* does not excuse one's refusal to advance, however, one's refusal to learn! Consequences apply to those who choose to learn. Different repercussions apply to those who refuse. Refusal to learn is the conscious wish to exist as though an animal, where perceptions trigger responsive actions automatically. It is the hope for a cognitive shortcut, a wish for emotional gratification. (E.g., *'It must be because I want it to be.'*) It cannot be thus, however, because Man is not so equipped, and subconscious mind knows it.

Correspondent with Creator's most gracious *Law of Allowance*, there also exists Creators *Law of Just Consequence*, wherein 'just' means exact. It is very simple. Abuse the *Law of Allowance*, and you will reap what you sow. Those who attempt, or pretend to themselves, that they can exist in adulthood by relying on (nature's) bridging pathway provided for children, will suffer.

Adolescence, offers a prime example of a maturing mind being forced to endure unwanted hardship. Much teenage rebellion, reveals desperate striving to engage full consciousness, to assert independence from authoritative domination and control. Teens generally want to accept life's responsibilities, to grow, and mature. Their will is smashed, however, when forced to abandon autonomy, to submit to parental, societal, authoritarian, or religious commandments. An emerging adult will very seldom grasp, that mental conformity, and strict subordination, are purposely intended to ensure his or her submission to authority. A further tragedy, is that most parents uphold submission to authority, because they are completely ignorant of their victimisation. Human anguish and trauma grow. Mental abandonment takes root, means for its correction remains unknown, while a fallacious mindset purporting moral correctness, is considered gospel truth to die for; exactly what authoritarian sociopaths fully intend.

The good news, is that every living adult is proof, and testament of Creator's gracious *Law of Allowance*. We have all used this law, and successfully programmed our subconscious minds. You and I, are the living proof of its veracity and unrivalled success.

No (purported) *laws* of Man have ever matched the gracious support of *allowance*, the forcefulness of *just consequence*, or both, and never will they! Together they present Creators *Law of Natural Justice*. Nothing surpasses, nor can it. Artificial laws can only trespass.

7

PROGRAMMING THE SUBCONSCIOUS MIND

Our nature impels that we think, and choose what will *add value to our life*. If we impress these *values* on our subconscious mind, with fervent resolution, it will prioritise them above all others. Such is not to teach subconscious mind its job. The object is to consciously affirm that a full and productive life is your chosen goal so that your two minds can work in synergistic harmony, and not at loggerheads with each other.

What follows is no mind game for idle or amusing indulgence. Robust fullness of your life is at stake, or great disappointment.

Three x One minute program

This program describes a method for programming one's subconscious mind. Other methods may substitute, but success will depend on *imagery* because that is the vocabulary of the subconscious mind. Next most important is one's fervent desire or will. Unless we definitively assert what we wish to accomplish, and *why most importantly*, the subconscious mind will not prioritise our desire above previously chosen, or accepted values, and so they will remain. Here is beauty and simplicity, for once the *why* of value assertiveness becomes one's life-upholding ethic, its regular practice becomes an assimilated habit, rather than an intrusion.

Below, is a method for impressing your chosen life-values on your subconscious mind. Do not take longer than one minute for each task. Keep it short and stay fully focussed. Half of one minute may be sufficient. If you cannot complete each task in one minute, revise its presentation and begin again next day. Subconscious mind wants information that is succinctly assertive. Lengthy descriptions imply laboured thought, incompleteness, perhaps a lack of sincerity.

Step 1 – Requesting your goal

Choose a very simple goal for your first programming exercise, e.g., *'I want to improve my health by enjoying a 20-minute walk each morning.'*

Note the accuracy, and value expressed. More than going for a walk, you want to enjoy it. You want to experience benefit, and feelings of joy. You want it for the reason of good health. That goal has a life-supporting value in it already. Notice the consciously chosen intention; namely, *I want to do this*. Observe the deliberate time slot. It's each morning, not just every day. Everything in that goal speaks of conscious, assertive intention. It holds a degree of passion, fervent desire, and will to uphold life.

Willed intention to act (1), passion (2), and upholding of life (3), should be the core components used in any, indeed all future value assignments. Aren't those exactly what you, as an infant, imparted to your subconscious mind when learning to crawl? Was your subconscious mind impressed? You bet!

Use these guidelines to frame your first subconscious programming exercise; recommended before bed.

1st Minute: Allocation and request:

Make your chosen value known to your subconscious mind, e.g., as per the example above.

Each of the three core attributes will be inclusive. If not, then add whichever is missing. For example, I want to achieve— (specify exactly what). My particular reasons are— (specify the life-value it will bring you). I'm committed to this achievement, and my life's betterment.

Vocally request assistance from your subconscious mind. Make a connection. Say words like, *'I'm seeking your help.'* Or, *'with my earnest desire, we will do this.'* Use your words.

KEY ATTRIBUTES: Will, intention, passion, life-benefit.

Step 2 - Visualise acting out your goal

During the second minute, mentally picture yourself doing what your goal expresses. Visualisation will adapt your goal to the (image) vocabulary of your subconscious mind, to which it is most receptive. The infant, in my example, could not ask to be there, so it looked there repeatedly, which pictorially impressed *there*, on the subconscious mind, thus the infant's desire to be *there*. Subconscious mind grasped passioned intent from repetitive visualisation.

2nd Minute: Visualise your actions

Picture yourself doing what you goal expresses you will do. Be legitimate, genuine and truthful. Visualise doing what you intend. Mentally see your desires transmuting into your subconscious mind as you shift from one image to the next. Visualising is important, regardless of how vividly real your mental pictures might be. See yourself waking at 5.45am, as birds sing outside your window, for example. Then dressing to go walking on the beach, or in the park, Picture this preparation as fun and excitement. Picture removing your shoes, the joyful touch of cool sand under your feet, and the feeling of nature coursing through your body as you deeply inhale fresh morning air. Picture enjoying a warm glow of satisfaction as refreshing water washes over your feet or body. Envisage revelling in nature, all cares gone. View improved health flowing through every part of your body.

Picture it all as actually happening. Relish feelings of happy emotions, and spring in your steps.

Stop after one minute. Don't over do it. Be convincing, never pleading.

KEY ATTRIBUTES: Visualised commitment, benefit, passion

You're presenting subconscious mind with a *painted picture of passioned intent,* using your own brush strokes of clarity. You're showing it your picture, and impressing it upon its library of images. You're brimming with passioned intention to really do it. This confirms your conscious will, and that subconscious mind has the power, and that one, without the other, is near useless. Thus, full conscious co-operation will progressively become the benchmark in your life; soon to become habitual.

Step 3 - Picture your goal as accomplished

For this 3rd minute, picture your goal as accomplished; see its materialisation, or manifestation in your life.

3rd Minute: Visualise Triumphant success

Vibrantly picture the manifestation of your assignment as complete in all respects; nothing omitted.

Visualise health amassing in your body, driving every negation out, just as your subconscious mind does. Picture gradual improvements in your life; e.g., revulsion of junk food. Picture warm emotions, an affirmation that your goal supremely corresponds with the fullness of your life, and that your emotional mentor agrees. Picture how your improved health will assist in everything that you do, listening, laughing, teaching, driving, sex, cooking.

Picture rejoicing. Express thanks to your subconscious partner for its assistance in achieving your prized goal. Conclude by asking sub-conscious mind to please awaken you, at your specified time, raring to go! Thank it for listening, and bid it goodnight.

KEY ATTRIBUTES: Visualise manifestation, express gratitude, give a time slot, closure.

That's it; your first *three step x one minute program* is all done. Have no doubts that the outcome you've willed, will indeed happen, absolutely none! Your subconscious mind has the power, and you've given it your passionate blessing to achieve all that *you've pictured in your conscious mind.*

Passioned commitment to advance your life, your valued reasons why that should happen, and your determination to make it happen, are altogether what triggers your subconscious mind to concur and oblige!

There are no shortcuts and no diversions. Your subconscious mind will accept any and all hesitations, discrepancies, confusions, doubts, unresolved dichotomies, unvalidated beliefs, or reservations as to what you most value. Every distraction will fail your goals. Every *hope* that subconscious mind *might work* will block it.

This program is not about hope, wishes or desires. It is about committed, passioned, wilful intention, and nothing less. You are fully on your own, in full conscious charge of your life, exactly as Creator intended. Creator backs your stand in the wholesomeness of your nature and being. You've been truly blessed with intellectual capacity to separate the truthfulness of life, from its belligerent and oppressive opposite, and you've chosen to live to the fullest.

For your subconscious mind to fully grasp and uphold your choice, and your passion, you really must follow through. You must do what you've impassioned that it should do! You can cheat your cognitive self. You can lie to yourself, and your subconscious mind will accept all such deceptions as truth. If you fail to honour your expressed desires, and intentions, it will accept that lying, falsity and lack of integrity are what you truly value.

Set your alarm clock 5 minutes past your start time, not just in case, but to further convince subconscious mind that you are totally committed. You want that subconscious mind should awaken you, not your clock. If your clock awakens you, then repeat the *three x one* exercise again, that night, and fully commit. (Before long, you'll donate your clock to a charity.)

Caution is warranted. Truth offers progress. Lies advance hindrance. Whatever relies on erroneous beliefs, that we might be implored to accept as knowledgeable understanding, is vacant in life terms. Non-substantive data cannot add anything of value to one's life. Use utmost caution at all times. Past programming, from childhood, or from many experiences since, not forgetting social pressures, will urge you to nominate life-values that accord with those of others, or confirm those you've already assimilated. Values change as your life advances, and so your subconscious mind needs periodic updating. Ask yourself, is this indeed what I value now? Am I hanging on to values that I've been shown, or taught that are necessary in life, or that served me as a teenager, but no longer? Am I in control of my life, and if not, why not?

It should be self-evident by now, that one should practice what they preach to their subconscious mind. Actions, are ultimately what subconscious mind monitors, not wishes, fanciful ideas, or mental content, save as to prick your conscience.

The 4P program – Practice to Prove – Polish to Perfect

The *3 step one minute program* is followed by practicing the **4P** *program*.

Your subconscious mind will very quickly grasp, and establish as (predominant) values, those which you most fervently practice. Awaken each day charged with the desire to make every minute count. Chalk up two or three successes using the *three step program*, and you'll have substantive evidence that you've programmed your subconscious mind, with your *life-values*, to the exclusion of pretenders, and imposters. Choosing valued goals will become second nature. Any fear of independence you may have had, will have long vanished.

Having Practised the technique, and Proven it, now Polish and Perfect it

When you begin to experience a warm glow in your heart, each time when reminded of a particular *value in life*, express gratitude to your subconscious mind. Foster this back and forth dialogue. Agree that when something hinders your goal, and you feel it, commonly called a negative emotion, that what you feel is still positive news. Learn from it. That's why subconscious mind delivered it.

Develop and nurture conversational communion between your two minds, as two loving partners do, each independent of mind, but alike in purpose, direction and value. Read your feelings, and respond to your subconscious mind. Polish this back and forth communion until it glows within you. Never forget that subconscious mind deals in the positive vein. It hears your gripes, and your grizzles, but won't act to fix them, until you freely commit.

You will have Polished the technique.

Be ever thankful and learn to treat mistakes as a positive lesson. Become excited by your achievements, enamoured to seek more from the same method, even to searching, and foreseeing wider implications you can begin practising. Be very grateful for what you've mastered, and that you alone did it. Be delighted, that you're spending less than one quarter the mental energy most folk waste undoing emotional stress, chaos, trauma's, and confusions they suffer.

Deconstructing your feelings will become an absolute breeze. The more accomplished you become, the more this beautiful, gracious, and simple exchange is polished! It has no equal! Never let go of this masterful blessing in your life.

With a full clarity of mind, and with absolute certainty, relish your knowledge, not faiths. Be overjoyed that you have indeed mastered your conscious mind, to the full agreement of your subconscious mind. Rejoice in their communion, and keep polishing it.

You've instilled *values of your choice*, so your *answers are within*, not outside. Go within. Your two minds are in complete unison and harmony, because that's what you desired. Now your success is their passion, and they have the blessed ability to deliver. Feel that warmth, and beauty, deep in your heart. Understand your love of spirit, and its love for you. It is you.

Lovingly grasp hold of *spiritually experiencing your whole self*. Be ever mindful of your absolute completeness, your wholesome, beautiful, unique, spiritual individuality. Love that your mind(s) know who you are, and that they agree! Be graciously and humbly thankful. Prize understanding that you are master of your destiny, maker of your soul, and be abundantly glad! Offer thanks to your Creator, with sincere, and loving reverence.

You will have Perfected the technique.

Mastery of one's self, accords all others the same opportunity. Self-mastery, is in this sense a moral discipline, because where the rights of all other singular beings are respected, no one can offend another by any application of his own. The principle, of suffering no unnecessary offence because one is careful to give none, extends to all.

Does it seem right that such manners, and respect, could substitute for what we call *law*; that such etiquette, or ethics, might benefit society, and preclude conflicts where today's so-called laws cannot even reach, much less resolve?

Whereas nature herself, has already bestowed every individual with the laws of their independent nature, such orderliness, and unified social communion, is the objective of natural law, in full play.

8

FEELINGS AND EMOTIONS

Value is *content*—not *process*

If we think of food as a *body-value*, then it's clear, that *value* is separate from the digestive *process*. Food delivers its true *value*, only after the digestive process has completed. *Value* is content, therefore, not process. *Content* is changeable, but the *process* is not. This fact is indisputable.

The subconscious mind is in a state of constant flux. Data content changes every millisecond, as it monitors every cell in your body, every eye movement, and every muscle twitch, but the natural process of handling that information remains governed. Consequently, we all have the ability to alter the content processed by our conscious and subconscious minds. That, exactly, is our ability to learn and grow, intellectually, emotionally and spiritually.

Could these simple lessons of value analysis, and correspondence, be taught to 5-year-old kids? Absolutely! Even earlier, particularly given the first few years of life are of crucial importance.

> If in any two years of adult life, men could learn as much as an infant learns in his first two years, they would have the capacity of genius. —Ayn Rand

Could this lesson be the study foundation for every other subject? Unmistakably! Every facet of life, from fishing to fashion, includes in some way, the reciprocal value process of conscious and sub-conscious communion.

Omniscience, or infallibility are not demanded. By the natural *Law of Allowance*, subconscious mind asks only that one chooses important *life-values* within the limits of one's present knowledge and understanding. Emotions exist to prompt expansion of our knowledge and values.

Subconscious mind wants you to express your actions, and your goals, in ethical, moral, and life sustaining spiritual terms, not your bank account. It wants that you master you, not for pets, possessions, position, money, dogmas, beliefs, governments, or ideologies to own you.

Whosoever ignores, or refuses subconscious mind's fervent pleas to be assigned values, will discover that *natural justice will serve their refusal*. Unwanted, hurtful, physical, mental, emotional, and spiritual consequences will ensue. No escape routes exist.

Image matching

Who remembers comparing two, near identical pictures side by side, to find several concealed discrepancies? That analogy best describes what subconscious mind does, when forming emotions. It compares the picture of your valued intentions, with the picture it sees via your senses, of what is happening in every present moment of your life. It does what all smart kids do. It puts one picture over the other, and holds both to the light so that mismatches appear in a flash.

Perfect matches trigger feelings of success. Discrepancies trigger feelings of dissatisfaction, or hindrance. Several anomalies may cause several different emotions, while emotional intensity is often caused by several corroborating matches (or mis–matches), rather than by one. The subconscious mind must use this image-matching process, because it has no ability to enquire, choose, or judge. Neither can it use conscious mind's (coneptual) word vocabulary. Nevertheless, images facilitate handling of incomprehensibly large amounts of data.

> Your subconscious is like a computer—more complex a computer than men can build—and its main function is the integration of your ideas. Who programs it? Your conscious mind. If you default, if you don't reach any firm convictions, your subconscious is programmed by chance— and you deliver yourself into the power of ideas you do not know you have accepted. But one way or the other, your computer gives you print-outs, daily and hourly, in the form of emotions—that are lightning-like estimates of the things around you, calculated according to your values. If you programmed your computer by conscious thinking, you know the nature of your values and emotions. If you didn't, you don't. —Ayn Rand[v]

Feelings

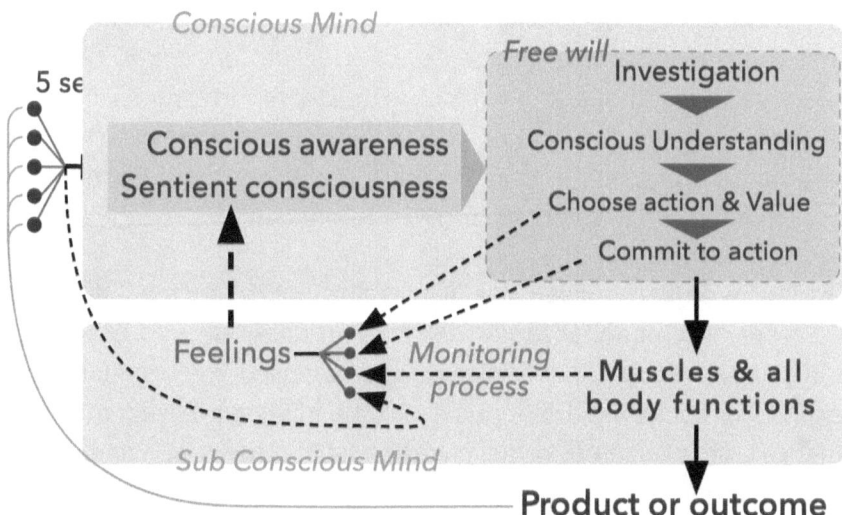

12 - Subconscious monitoring

Dotted lines in diagram 12, show four pathways out of which feelings are formed.

One's actions, and one's environment are monitored, through the five senses, exactly as perceiving a thing, or an event initially. Information from within the body is watched, and added, including the values one has chosen, and of course, one's present moment actions. Feelings form thereby. They are delivered to sentient consciousness, thereby completing the triple sequential process.

Feelings are an abstraction, therefore, just like word concepts and perceptions, are abstractions. Although subconscious mind integrates data from many sources, it offers no explanation as to what causes a feeling. Neither feelings, nor emotions, explain their source. They cannot communicate words, because they are an abstracted sentient image, despite being complete in all respects. Emotions serve little value, without choosing to enquire, so to understand them, then acting according to that understanding.

Deconstructing feelings

Deconstructing an emotion means to search, to find the value that it supports, or challenges. Assert *your chosen values*, on your subconscious mind, and it will authentically report your success, or distress, via feelings that *echo your values*. If the mood pleases, you will name it according to its felt intensity. If not, you will name it according to the intensity of displeasure you suffer.

We put words to our feelings. It is entirely our choice whether we consider an emotional report distracts, irritates, annoys, or angers. Otherwise, we decide whether we are bemused, interested, happy, excited, or overjoyed. Feelings can also be intuitively based, meaning that what has angered, or delighted oneself in the past, will assume the same named-response for a similar present moment event.

Many will disagree, vehemently so, likely saying, *'but I know instinctively whether I'm irritated, happy, delighted or ticked off. My feelings are real. They leave no doubt about how I feel! How can you say that I don't know what I feel, when you can't even feel, what I feel?'*

Feelings prompt us to consciously trace their cause, to learn, and to profit from our actions and activities. Those firmly convinced that feelings arrive already named, and explained, will see no need to investigate their root cause. Conscious discovery is thereby short-circuited. In short, these folk indulge in (non-thinking) re–action, instead of (cognitive) response–ability.

Many, who consider investigation of their feelings to be an onerous task, or imposition, will complain. Likely they will say; *'My feelings leave no doubt, about how I feel.'* For these folk, feelings are explanations, alerts. They feel hurt, and so they seek to escape by the quickest route possible. Nature will not be cheated, however.

Every emotion poses questions. *What truth is for me to discover? What can I learn from this feeling?* The cause of feelings, arising from falling into a creek while attempting to leap over it, are seldom found in the mishap. The fall clearly triggered the emotion, most certainly, but the mishap does not explain one's feeling, misfortune, annoyance, frustration, or self-reproach, or why those feelings differ. Enquiry might point to wasted time, for example, ruined clothing, missing a bus to meet a friend, being late for an appointment, or a thousand other reasons. All distractions aside, the source of the feeling lies in understanding *what value,* was to be gained by successfully jumping the creek.

What *value* was threatened, by the fact of missing an appointment, for example? Was it an interview for a new job, or a hairdresser appointment? What value did the new job potentially bring to one's life, or what benefit did a fine coiffure proffer? Discovering thwarted values, is a no-brainer for the above example and many similar, but for more complex matters, the path will not be so apparent.

We choose to give our life meaning. We each are responsible for the values we nominate. We are responsible for implanting values in our subconscious mind. Failure results in a stunted emotional faculty, one rendered almost useless. That explains why feelings are so often considered subjective, and outside conscious influence. So it is, for many people, that their emotional faculty, most precious amongst Creator's gifts, is put out of reach.

For one who conscientiously assigns values to their actions, respectful of their life, it will be relatively easy to reverse engineer one's emotions. They will ask what *life-value* upholds the feeling, whether that value is real, or false, should it be re-assessed, or should one act differently in future? Those who choose real values in life, and implant them, understand their emotions, because they programmed them. They understand how Creator's *Natural Law of Efficacy* (described later), works in practice, and they exploit it to the full.

Others, will find it very difficult to understand their emotions, if not impossible. First, they won't even know what a *life-value* is. They won't know how life-values are assigned to their subconscious mind, consciously, or by assimilation. Taught that subconscious mind is impervious to control, which is true, the question of how they might influence, but not control their subconscious mind, is never considered. They will not enquire further.

Feelings referred to as *subjective*, are not. Just because our subconscious mind has no words, does not prevent its image vocabulary from objectively informing, of a matter that needs the attention of our conscious mind. Feelings prompt conscious mind to explore, and understand the emotive message, in objective value-terms. They implore that we reverse engineer the feeling, so to discover which of our personal values led to it.

Introspection is the only way to reveal the objective truth behind feelings. Each enquiry must seek the truth, for only that will reveal whether the founding *value* premise of a particular emotion is true, or false. Having identified, and dealt with the causative *value*, the feeling usually vanishes. Its purpose is complete; but it may commit to memory so as to serve intuition.

Although feelings are most certainly definite, for so long as the cause is not understood, they cannot serve the valued purpose Creator intended. When conscious mind is starved understanding, so is one's progress in life.

Learning from feelings

Without a ruthlessly honest commitment to introspection, so as to identify the cause of a particular feeling, one will not discover what they sensibly feel, or why.

> Intense emotions can undermine a person's capacity for rational decision-making, even when the individual is aware of the need to make careful decisions— The authors draw on recent research that demonstrates that human decision-making is governed by two neural systems–the deliberative and the affective, or emotional. The latter, which the authors dub emote control, is much older, and served an adaptive role in early humans by helping them meet basic needs and identify and respond quickly to danger. As humans evolved, however, they developed the ability to consider the long-term consequences of their behavior and to weigh the costs and benefits of their choices.
>
> "Human behavior is not under the sole control of emotion or deliberation but results from the interaction of these two processes," Loewenstein said. — John M. Grohol, Psy.D.[vi]

That quotation sums all previously described. There is no clear-cut pathway to the origin of a feeling without first instilling *life-values* into the subconscious mind. One cannot know whether a particular emotion is an appropriate response, mistaken response, or a vicious illusion resulting from years of self-deception.

Those who shortcut value considerations, because *intellectual stuff is too hard, or is only for academics*, expose themselves to emotional trauma. They do not get off lightly. Ultimately they are obliged to mentally deal with every (emotion delivered) value consideration they've attempted to escape. Sadly, they've no idea where to begin.

No emotions are negative

Contrary to popular belief, there is no such thing as a *negative emotion*. Every emotion delivers positive news. Being informed that your mission is falling off the rails is not bad news; it is good news. You've been shown a warning light, so that you can trace the cause and fix the problem.

Intuit understanding plays a role, but truthfulness is vital. As previously discussed, intuition is a prior truth, or it is non-validated beliefs, or fallacies, brought into immediate focus. The same measure of truth, or falsity, may apply to feelings. The subconscious mind is not being untruthful. It is matching a present moment event, or circumstance, with *what conscious mind has previously informed it to be truth*. It cannot do other, because Creator has refused it any ability to differ, or make independent judgement.

Feelings - Mentoring faculty

Emotions, every one of them, serve as your protector. Although to be investigated and learned from, one is not required to investigate cause in that instant. Notwithstanding, feelings should be examined, if ever one desires to learn what causes their joy or sorrow.

Those who do will win. Others are ruled by their emotions. Sufferance, for better or worse, is everyone's choice. Difference is the initial choosing, or refusing of values, after that, choosing or refusing to enquire the root value abstractly contained within one's feelings. The common sense of it is straightforward, and beautiful. Just as Man's body has an immune system working to eradicate and clean out any harmful matter, so Man's emotion faculty advocates mental clean-outs, or retentions.

You are the author of the *values* you implant in your subconscious mind. You are the author of your feelings. The conclusion is self-evident. *Emotions are Man's mentoring faculty.* The process enables one to learn, advance, prosper, and grow in mental, emotional, and spiritual maturity. Unless one commits to that understanding, and lives it, nothing is gained. Who teaches today that conscience and emotions are Man's mentoring faculty? No one does. Who is deprived as a result?

Conscience

Conscience, is the (intuitively automated) faculty that assists in distinguishing right from wrong. Since Mans life is the fundamental determinant, then consistent assessment, and appraisal of values respectful of one's life, should produce a self-sustaining ethic. Conscience will then advise of life's advancements, or regressions. Accordingly, Man has two parallel systems reporting on his well-being, being conscience and emotional mentoring.

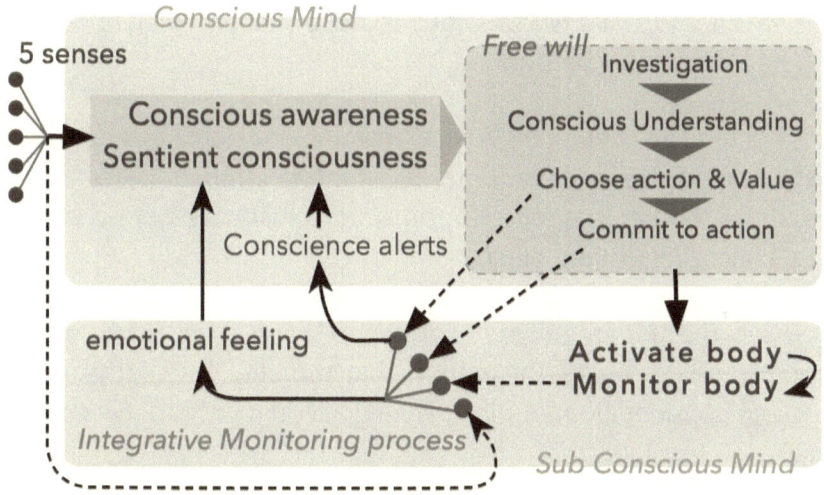

13 – Conscience and emotions

Value choices, assessed by the subconscious mind before any action, are delivered as *'conscience alerts'* to one's conscious mind. In diagram 13, the process from sensory stimuli, clockwise to the point of choosing an action, was previously described. So was the process of value assessment. The emotional faculty—bottom left—integrates information from four sources, as shown by dashed lines in the diagram, all as previously explained.

Observe how conscience differs from emotions. The reason is that *value assessments* directly prompt one's conscience, while emotions additionally rely on integrated data from three other sources.

After one has acted, multiple data is collected from three additional sources concerning that action. All are integrated and *delivered as feelings* to one's sentient consciousness.

Conscience vs Emotions

In short—

- *Conscience,* alerts conscious mind to *pay strict (thought) attention to one's life-values*; one's ethics.
- *Emotion,* alerts conscious mind of *actions that uphold or trespass chosen values*.

It is not until an action takes place, that any emotional feeling can be experienced. This is because three, of the four inputs necessary for emotions to form, are reliant upon actions that have not yet begun. The conclusion is very clear.

You are the author of your conscience, and your morality. This understanding, belies the notion that morality is a social order, societal consideration, or ethic. Taking account of both, we can see that—

- Conscience, delivers value-prompts *prior an event or action.*
- Feelings, deliver value-prompts *subsequent an event or action.*

Whatsoever may conflict with one's values, will prick conscience before an action, while feelings will objectively report on any moral conflict, following an action. Note that pangs of conscience may occur in tandem with emotions, e.g., one can be emotionally satisfied that an action has succeeded, yet feel guilty for having done it.

In summary, our whole being is (auto) monitored every moment of every day, our free choices accepted and upheld, whether based in truth, or not. The conscious mind is alerted of value discrepancies before actions, and afterwards, all measured against the *value* of life, including respect, or disrespect of others right to their life.

It follows that morals are the (free will) *enacted* practice of every individual's self-chosen *ethics*; or lack thereof, respective of their life. (This conclusion is expanded later.)

This process, and faculties exist within every man woman and child, all automated by the subconscious mind, all fueled by free will choices, respective of one's chosen ethics and 'life-values.' In all, this is Mans alerting and mentoring faculty, endowed by Creator for ethically sustaining the process of living, whether alone on a remote island, or in society.

Thus hails a complete overhaul and re-appraisal of *conscience*—the science and practice of *ethics*—all human and social sciences.

9

FROM OBJECTIVITY TO SPIRITUALITY

Every man, woman, and teenager on earth, can advise subconscious mind of value choices. Mature individual's may learn of its appraisals, through conscience, and emotions, if they so choose. Two-way communication, between our conscious and subconscious minds, is available to adolescents and adults, all administered by free will choice.

Data must transfer from the subconscious *image* vocabulary to the (fee will) *conceptual* vocabulary, and return again to *images*, for the 'sequential process' to complete. Creator's plan for Man is equally as beautiful in concept, and in structure, as it is acutely precise in accomplishment.

> Science, in only the last 10 or 15 years, is recognising that Mans brain has far greater capabilities than have ever been credited. Moreover the associative elements of mind, consciousness, subconsciousness and emotional interactions are only now being seen in their fullness

> Neuroscience research tells us that much of the brain is constructed to support "automatic" processes–that are faster than conscious deliberations and that occur with little or no awareness or feeling of effort.

Research also tells us that our behaviour is under the pervasive and often unrecognised influence of "affective" (emotion) systems that are absolutely essential for daily functioning.

So our behaviour emerges from the interplay between controlled (conscious) and automatic systems on the one hand, and between cognitive (reason) and affective (emotion) systems on the other. —SMH[vii]

That quotation, surprisingly from an article concerning economics, endorses the *sequential process* as described. To instil (chosen) values in subconscious mind, first they must be converted from words into images. Subsequently, feelings in a (visually) sentient form must be changed back into the conceptual word vocabulary if we are to learn from them. Free will is involved in both directions; to the subconscious mind, and back from it.

This interchange, is Creator's lesson representing a diversity of thoughts and actions among equals, or one's likes. This offers an example of value exchange between individuals of different countries, races and cultures. Creator has most pertinently, and logically, modelled lessons of diversity in Man's value-monitoring system.

This *interplay,* is what the last sentence of the above quotation denotes, in effect.

Man's triple intellectual process offers three different expressions—

- *Subconscious,* to *Conscious,* back to *Subconscious*—or as—
- *Image* data to *Concept* data, then back to *Image* data—or
- Automatic perception (*fast*), thence free will deliberation (*slow*), thence automatic feelings (*fast*).

The subconscious mind cannot mentor your life, even as it monitors every aspect of your body, without you advising what *value* you've chosen to place on your life and your actions. Observe, that at a traffic accident, a police officer, ambulance attendant, bystander, tow truck driver, distraught relatives, and news reporter, will all have different emotions, yet all are visually witnessing the same event. They all have separate *values*, respectful of that event.

If, for any given action, a particular condition supports what you've chosen to achieve, you'll have a warm glowing feeling of some degree. To the extent that you feel it, you will name it, even intuitively, based on prior knowledge. If a feeling reports an unfavourable condition, you'll find a sad, or melancholy name that fits the intensity of what you experience. The name you put to an emotional feeling, should be the word concept best reflecting the depth of what value is satisfied, or hindered.

Objective Intent

Feelings are not subjective, as most folks believe. They are nature's method of objectively informing your progress or life's hindrances. Objectivity works sequentially.

1.   One objectively decides what action(s) they will pursue.
2.   *He or she, places an objective life-supporting value on that choice. (If not, the subconscious mind automatically defaults to a prior value.)*
3.   He or she, objectively commits to that action.
4.   Subconscious mind initiates muscle activity to complete the action, then objectively monitors its material progress.
5.   Subconscious mind objectively checks, and evaluates its *value-laden* progress.
6.   Subconscious mind integrates the data, then submits status reports as feelings—sentient images.
7.   *Conscious mind, chooses to accurately and objectively investigate the (abstracted) feeling-report, to learn of its advice.*

Subjectivists omit items two and seven, because they believe that subconscious mind cannot be influenced objectively, whereby all feelings are subjective.

Objectivists include items two and seven, because they know with certainty, that *objectively chosen values* program one's subconscious mind, whereby resultant emotions are *objective*.

To exercise full consciousness, in *life-value* terms, is the greatest reverence and gratitude anyone can offer Creator. Whoever attains this level of conscious enlightenment, will experience a load lifting off their shoulders. They will realise they've nothing to gain from pseudo-intellectuals, new-age mystics, pretenders, imposters, blood spilling authority, and soul destroying spiritual bandits. All predators are blasted into oblivion for eternity! Every soul destroying intruder puffed with egotistic belligerence will hit a brick wall—one's dynamic, impenetrable, whole, material, mental, and spiritual self!

Those who discover their beautiful spiritual aspects, will also learn a profound truth. Every emotional chaos, or trauma, formidably originating from pulpits and parliaments of fiction, falsity, and irrelevance, will have been struck out of their life, without them even asking!

Spiritual independence, enlightenment, and empowerment, will manifest as never before. The world will present in a whole new light.

As you become more accomplished with the *3 x 1,* and *4P* programs, over time your subconscious mind will begin dropping (image) hints concerning even more things you might do to assist your life. These (intuitive) hints will found on goals and values you've previously impressed on your subconscious mind, and that now have been committed to memory. It's very simple. Subconscious mind compares one, or more of your value images with what it is monitoring through your five senses, and reports results of this match. You receive an intuitively sensitive, spiritual feeling.

So it is that you can begin asking subconscious mind, for ideas and suggestions concerning how important life-goals might result.

Mind communion is not a passive meditation technique, where one divorces from intellectual thought, allowing (subjective) information to flow. Instead, it is a deliberate, conscious request, asking that subconscious mind use its *image matching capacity* to reach beyond your cognitive, investigative ability. Please understand this fully. It is vital. You are not submitting to all and sundry suggestions; to impulses, or energies of all kind. You are deliberately requesting information from a source that is entirely devoted to your life's success! We're talking now, of spiritual communion.

Remembering that subconscious mind cannot work in a vacuum, so conscious requests of this kind must focus on a particular passioned desire, to attain a life-supporting goal. It should entreat that subconscious mind discover, and present image information that your conscious mind cannot find, or has not yet found.

When answers begin popping into your head, know for certain that your two minds are indeed in full communion, united in service of a spiritual being, *spiritually living* in a materialistic environment.

All that remains is to authenticate, or validate these (image) hints, then transform the answers into the practicalities of your life. Polish this technique, and outstanding results will flow.

Whole and Indivisible

Man is more powerfully creative than many think. Do not be surprised when you find yourself asking, why wasn't I taught this as a kid? What will you teach your children? Who else better than a parent who has learned self-mastery and spiritual fulfilment?

Preceding chapters have described the fulness of Mans body, mental, emotional, and spiritual aspects, from a completely new perspective.

Free will has proper place and function. Mans six higher faculties have been re-appraised in the context of a *triple sequential process*.

Diagram 14 encapsulates all shown previously. It shows Mans entire mental, and emotional processes. Beginning with existence, at the bottom left, and tracing clockwise, thick black arrows lead to actions at bottom right. Subconscious perception, delivered to conscious mind, prompts free will to explore the discovery process, (top right), resulting in cognitive understanding. Consideration given to proposed actions, includes value assessments, that, whether consciously assigned, or subconsciously assimilated, will affect both conscience and emotions.

Feelings, delivered to one's sentient awareness, are available for free will investigation and learning. Intuition, describes Creators *Law of Efficacy*, provided that its memory database is factual and not fictional. Four sources fuel the emotive process, as prior described, and knowledge consigns to memory. Creator's *Law of Allowance* permits infants to experience their free will, and full emotions, while their cognitive minds develop over time.

Lazy or apathetic minds, who choose to shortcut cognitive discovery, or value assessment, are exposed to the *Natural Law of Just Consequence*, including emotional traumas. Instinctual safety protection bypasses free will enquiry, instantaneously activated by memory, and monitoring, both automatic subconscious functions. The full process is sequential, orderly and complete, although each individuated function performs independently. Man's physical, intellectual, and emotional processes, are brimming over with natural laws. Not one commands free will!

Thus the full sequential mental process reveals itself. Nothing in Man's history, indeed all human science, has ever attempted to portray our faculties in such manner. Why? Because Man is not considered an end in him/herself, instead a contributing cog in the wheel of society, to which (s)he is always beholden.

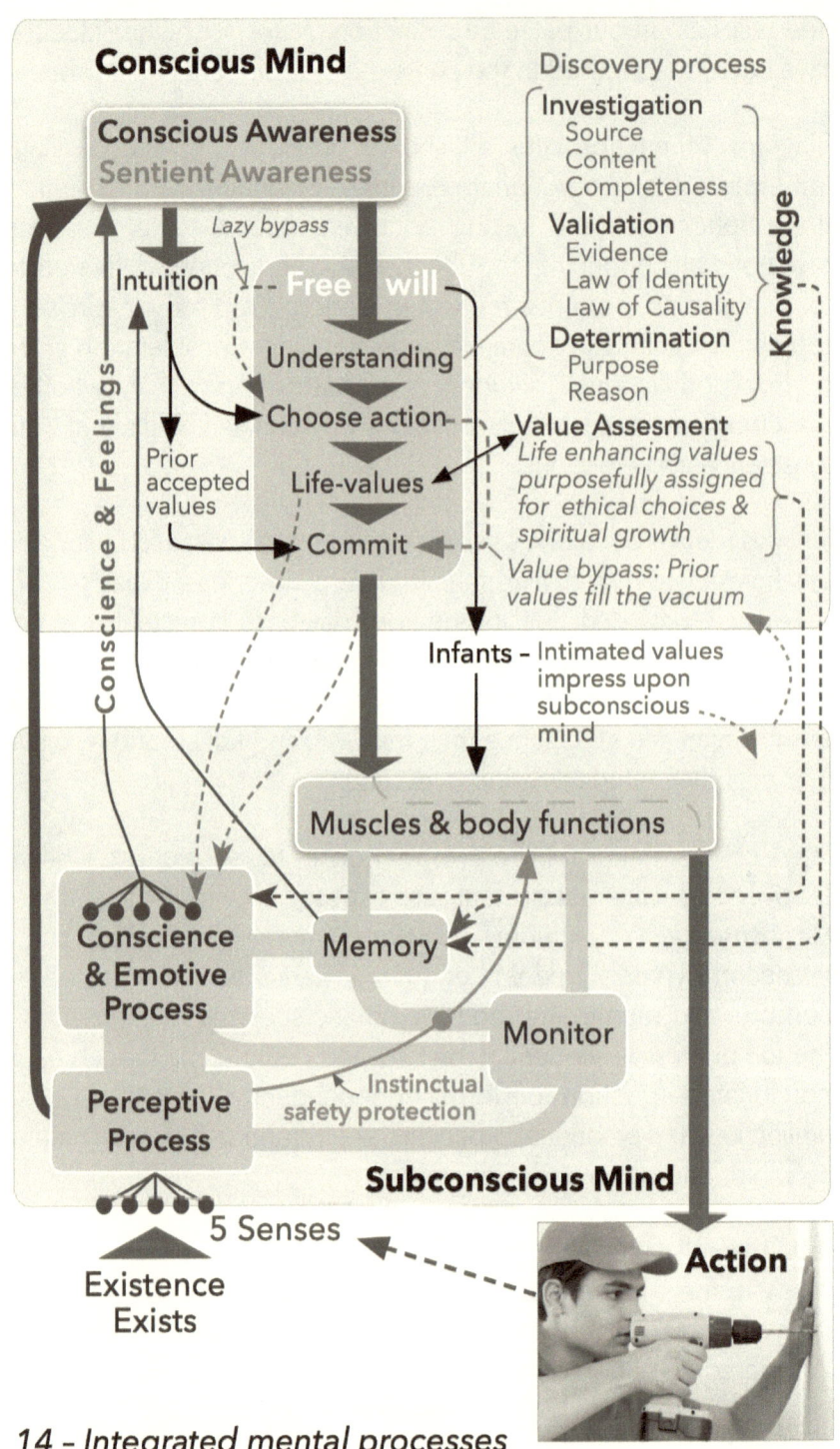

14 - Integrated mental processes

Study diagram 14 and you'll see clockwise circuits, within circuits, and that *escape routes* invariably invoke dire consequence. The subconscious mind is a contiguous, interconnected, all encompassing entity, having two entry points only—Mans conscious agreement and value choices, plus Creator's *natural Law of Allowance*. (Infant understanding is bypassed without penalty.) No shortcuts exist but what Creator has allowed.

The subconscious mind is no longer *beyond reach*. It supports life to the degree we consciously support it. Values are shown to have vital significance in life-terms, pivotal to conscience, emotions and mentoring. Ethics are rescued from business practices and restored to proper function in personal decision making, allied with value determination. Morality has been snatched from the collective, and returned to each independent living being, contrary to today's teachings. Creators *Law of Allowance* corresponds with its checkmate, the *Law of Just Consequence*. Together they comprise the *Law of Natural Justice*.

Man's six higher faculties are addressed within the totality of the *sequential process*. Diagram 17 comprehensively portrays Mans mental, and emotional being, as never before.

Free will – In charge

Aside from instinctual, reflex, protective actions, free will is entirely in charge and is responsible for all outcomes; material, ethical, moral and spiritual. It is not free to alter its process, or the laws of its nature, but is free to abuse them, e.g. refuse to think, or accept erroneous faiths, and superstitions, as knowledge. Free will is not a *free license*. It is the freedom to think and act—but not with impunity. *Just consequences* cannot be avoided. Every (beneficial or detrimental) outcome belongs to its initiator, or perpetrator, with no exceptions, which is *Natural Justice*.

Spirituality and interactive communion

It should now be evident that what Creator decreed as (existent) Law, and Man subsequently decrees (to be) law, are vastly different. This astute observation has profound implications—

> Without the hypothesis of a divine legislator, who for some unfathomable reason prefers to encrypt his commands in nature, theories of *'Leges naturales'* (Natural Law) get nowhere–and with that hypothesis, non-believers can only conclude that they are conjured up out of thin air.—Frank van Dun [12]

The (very fathomable) reason, I submit, why *'a divine legislator prefers to encrypt his commands in nature,'* is so that no other legislator could ever erase His legislation. Let's explore this notion.

Image transfer, confirms success of the *three-step one minute* program. It establishes that one's two minds are in full concert agreement. One's passion and desire to fully live has been transmitted, and received, as a *spiritually abstracted expression of the conscious mind.* Subconscious mind has gratefully accepted one's values, as *consciously chosen, spiritual fuel.* Later, in return, subconscious mind delivers an *abstracted expression* of success, or distress, concerning attainment of that *spiritual value.*

Do you see the magnificence of this *spiritual communication* between your two minds? Both to-and-from communications embrace the fullness of your life *according to your chosen values.* You are in complete (conscious) control of your physical, mental and spiritual worlds! You are living in exact accord with Creator's desires. Better yet by so living, you reverence your creation and Creator, often expressed by the phrase, *action speaks louder than words.*

By the methods described, you have learned how to adapt nature to your needs, physically, mentally and spiritually. You fully understand that *you are a spiritual being, living a spiritual life,* on a physical plane. You feel utterly blessed and so you should.

- Does that explain why Creator, as 'divine legislator,' would encrypt his commands in nature, and so forbid removal?
- Does that explain why neither one of your minds can be permitted to corrupt the other?
- Does that explain why every notion, idea, philosophy, belief or emotional fancy, must receive your conscious approval as truth; meaning *accepted for value?*

If spiritual life means a way of life conducive of the most integrated and wholesome, life-enhancing human functioning and behaviour, then to be *fully Man, is to be spiritual.* Spirituality speaks of independence, and uniqueness, not submission to collective rule. Neither is spirituality dependent upon some deity, theology, salvation, ascended guru, or any other invention of Man.

Unbounded fullness of your life, is the ultimate joy that Creator intended. You are its sole facilitator. Every means is yours, yet it remains, that the fullness of being is reliant upon your activation, of you. Only your thoughts and actions will adapt (real) nature to your purpose as Creator intended. Your life is in your mind, and hands, and there are no shortcuts. Mans integrity, is his devotion to life, others reciprocally. In summarised form, that is Creator's *Natural Law of Integrity*, as a life-value, intrinsic within the natural laws of his being. It is to be learned, but sadly, is not taught today.

Spirituality & Science

Scientists very often dismiss the existence of spirit, because it doesn't exist in their realm of tangible facts. In their minds, therefore, Man's spirit cannot live. Important matters of the soul are inconsequential; everything thence treated as purely material cause and effect.

Spirituality does not grow out of conscious content; instead, the spiritual communion between conscious and subconscious minds as described above. It is their harmony, co-operation, grace, and reverence for each other. The result will be self-growth, self-respect, self-mastery, self-esteem, and mutual devotion to a life truly lived.

Science does not grow out of spirituality either. It is the process of exploration, discovery, relationships and ideas in the material world. These may translate into spiritual terms—values that aid and support Man's physical and spiritual self, as a fully integrated homogenous living being.

Thus, it is not the role of science, to interpret its achievements in spiritual terms. Instead, it is for each to learn from scientific enquiry, grasp *life-values* and use them, so to discover and exercise their spiritual essence. Natural laws forbid this *sequential process* be reversed. Science should not condemn spiritual values, therefore. Science should spark spiritual discovery, much as perception sparks cognitive discovery.

The most eloquent truth is the simplest.

Subconscious mind is devoted to your life succeeding, and growing in the spiritual sense, whereby your choice to consciously and consistently pursue the same objective is its most perfect accompaniment!

Natural laws are simple, easily understood, immutable, and just. Fortunately, and only very recently, science is recognising that its affinity with spirituality is undeniable, exactly as conscious and subconscious minds are profoundly interactive. Philosophers, and spiritual teachers should assist this enlightenment, but seldom do they. They've yet to grasp that spirit interfaces physicality within Mans nature, and that spirituality is nurturance of their communion.

Nothing excels for Man, is more direct, or more efficacious. Nothing but the full exercise of your faculties, pays tribute to you, your spiritual essence, and your Creator more reverently.

This best explains Man as *a spiritual being, living a spiritual life,* in a physical domain.

10

PREFACE TO NATURAL LAW

America's *founding fathers* came closest to ridding the scourge of a political collective. *Life, Liberty and the Pursuit of Happiness,* came close to ensuring Mans individual, unalienable rights as an independent living being, but fell short. This mention is not to criticise, but to add support to *individual rights* as ideal. The (US) 1776 *Declaration of Independence* divorced one state from another. Today's task is to divorce separate *living beings* from any *state*. Thomas Jefferson later agreed this was the context in which he drafted the Declaration of Independence.

The time has come for Man to honour this commitment to independent life, as Creator ordained.

No Trespass

There is no conflict between orderly governance (natural laws), and free will. Natural laws govern our mental process, and that means none can be permitted to interfere with, or corrupt the other. Exactly because they are differently independent, and yet co-dependent, one must never violate the other's function, or destruction of one's self, is inevitable. To violate another's right to life, is to sacrifice one's own. Reciprocal guarantee underscores all natural laws.

No man-made laws match this achievement, and never can they!

> For free content to coexist with natural law process, neither can be permitted to interfere with or corrupt the other. — Kenneth Bartle

Now join the dots. Translate these natural laws of Man, into a free society abiding the natural law.

> For free society to co-dependently function within natural law, each must guarantee non-violation of the other, or both will vanish. —Kenneth Bartle.

Creator's gift to mankind is beyond compare. The process of free choice cannot be interfered with, by any means whatsoever, but we can mentally process whatever we choose. We can advance or fail ourselves, but we cannot change the process.

Purposeful behaviour

From information in previous chapters, it is possible to draw objective, universal conclusions about Mans behaviour. The very fact that we engage in acts for a reason, implies that we have values, preferences, and choices; patterns of order or natural laws, inherent in our mental processes. These must be inescapably true, for any living human being who exhibits intentional thoughts, and actions.

Deductive study of human action, based on the premise that individual beings engage in purposeful behaviour, is *praxeology*. When a purposeful action is adopted, the source of its purpose is profoundly important. Accordingly, the study of law must begin with the natural-law concept of the individual human being, rather than the notion of Man as a human agent.

A country's politically based *Constitution* cannot answer to praxeology, because *rule-based society* rejects *individuality*, in favour of the *collective*. A (universal) *Constitution of Man*, that upholds and protects the individual rights of Man, is the only thing that will satisfy praxeology. For that, please see the *Constitution of Man* and its *Declaration of Individual Rights* in Chapter Twenty-two. That document testifies the desirability for a *Commission of Justice,* or equal, (example at naturalelaw.com). Such a commission, would exist to protect unalienable individual rights abiding the natural law, all based on the nature of Man.

> The thought of how far the human race [might] have advanced without government simply staggers the imagination. — Attributed to Doug Casey, 1979

Natural Law

Perhaps none better, or more succinctly describes Creator's natural laws, than this extract from Borden et. al. v State, and the words adopted by Justice Scott of the Supreme Court of Arkansas, in 1850-51:

> A Natural Law is defined—to be a rule which so necessarily agrees with the nature and state of man, that, without observing its maxims, the peace and happiness of society can never be preserved. These are called Natural Laws because a knowledge of them may be attained merely by the light of reason, from the fact of their essential agreeableness with the constitution of human nature.

When one grasps how natural laws sustain and enrich life, and desires to translate these laws into society, it is necessary to understand their ethical, moral, and spiritual essence. What are their founding principles and their relationships? Can they be expressed as core principles, perhaps like the ten commandments of Moses?

Indeed these principles do exist, and they can be expressed; but not as commandments. Here are the ten fundamentals upon which all natural laws are founded.

Natural law – Ten fundamental tenets

1 Natural Law is to be respected; not obeyed

Man's free will is always free! Natural law cannot be obeyed, or disobeyed. Every living man, woman and child have free will choice to respect natural law, treat it with belligerence, or contempt, even refuse it. Notwithstanding, all consequences that befall are one's own.

2 Natural law is of Man; not for Man

Integrity, honesty, commitment, truth, and self-preservation, are inherent in the natural laws that govern all our faculties, systems, and processes, without which life would cease. Because the content of free will mind is not so governed, Creator has endowed Man with a conscience, and an emotional faculty, that prompt and impel that Man should choose life supporting goals.

It follows that values, ethics, and morality, all emanate from within individual men and women, in every country and culture, each according to his or her choice, correspondent with the right of all others so to choose. Natural law cannot inform in the usual law-book fashion; rather is written by Creator within every man, woman, and child, as life-sustaining moral guidance.

3 Natural law is objective, not subjective

Natural laws exist to sustain every individual's life. Transfer these into Mans societal dealings with others, and not one thing changes. Subjective opinion is not refused, but is fundamentally irrelevant if it offers no spiritual, or life-sustaining purpose. Actions that respect natural law are objectively lawful, and serve justice, therefore. They uphold life objectively. Actions that do not, are unlawful, and unjust, mitigating circumstances admitted.

4 Natural law is immutable

Natural law is inviolate. It cannot be overruled by any Man, or any construct of Man, without self-confessing by such action, the unlawful power or force so to do.

5 Natural law upholds the individuality of human Life

We are not all one, as multitudes today proclaim. We are the aggregation of separate living beings, all equal by species, all independent by our uniqueness. No (common) lung, organ, brain, stomach, mind, or consciousness exists. Individuality of human life cannot fuse into one unified entity, else uniqueness, and one's unalienable right to life, are foregone.

6 Natural law grants no authority

The natural law permits no jurisdiction for one individual to command another. (This is testified by neither of our two minds being able to overrule the other.) The principle of integrity, and one's unalienable right to life, is evident. No one has authority to trespass upon another's life.

7 Natural law refuses all authority

Natural Law denies all orders, all authority save its own, whether from a partner, neighbour, pulpit, parliament, congress, or any other of any kind, without exception.

8 Natural law admits no trespass

Whosoever knowingly initiates the use of physical or coercive force, or fraud against others, negates and paralyses the victim's means of survival. Perpetrators, by their trespass action(s), abdicate the free-will right to choose. Outlaws are not free.

Natural law refuses initiated force, in all its forms, but reserves the moral right to use remedial power to arrest such assaults.

Expressed differently, two persons cannot be free and equal, when one of them is controlling, managing, threatening, blackmailing, or extorting the other. Crime is not committed by free persons, but by those who have wilfully sacrificed their autonomy. The full force of Natural Law is justly brought to bear upon the perpetrator, being the only force one has a right to choose. Natural justice binds criminal action, to one's choice to relinquish their freedom. No legal instrument, or purportedly lawful means, may preside contrary. All that attempt such, are unjust, and unlawful.

9 Natural law seeks integrity

Natural Law, and Positive Law, apply to different things, so cannot be alternative systems of rules applicable to the same thing. Natural orderliness, that governs Man's being, is complete and without lack, entirely given to the maintenance of one's life, with immutable, undivided, wholesome integrity. Man's physiology, his intellectual, mental, and emotional processes, are so governed, but the content of what they process, is not.

Natural law, obliges that Man acts in spiritual accordance with the same integrity of purpose that upholds his physical life. Spiritual integrity is vital, not only to preserving life, but to sustaining, and enhancing, inestimably bountiful joys that result from living a life of moral integrity!

10 The natural law supports one's life, respectful of all others

Integrity, lawfulness, and justice, are the foundation and culmination of natural law, the full expression, and manifestation of mind, body, and soul, having respect to life. When Mans actions outwardly manifest honesty, and integrity, found within, without which his mental and bodily life could not exist, so the orderliness, and completeness of Mans societal structures, will correspond. Not one thing more is needed, (save the arrest of violence), and nothing less will suffice.

Freedom or burden?

Those fundamentals, open the door to even greater understanding yet to come. Natural justice supports that Man is a being of self-made virtues, ethics, morality, satisfaction, and joy, and of self-made soul.

It remedies all incursions, yet, some lament that natural law seemingly holds them accountable for actions, as though an added burden. It simply is not so.

The *Natural Law of Allowance,* and the *Natural Law of Efficacy,* are fully supportive of life. The first allows growth at one's individual pace, while the second, acts like a turbocharger for those who choose it. Moreover, the *Law of Just Consequence* is not a burden to right thinking individuals. It beneficially rewards those who elect to live to the fullest. So where is the burden? There is none!

Free others, and one frees oneself, from perceived obligations that do not exist. Natural laws that uphold life are no burden! They are the pathway to freedom! That Man's spiritual being interfaces the material existence of life, means that his joy is to live, by transforming materialism to his soul's purpose. All else is a diversion from this goal.

Introducing the natural laws

Natural laws are not God's commandments. Given free will choice, the very notion of a commandment, is at once repressive and repulsive. Natural law is unavoidable. Every virtue has a consequence, and every trespass of virtue has a consequence. Fortunately, every man and woman have free choice to know in advance of any action, exactly what potential outcome will result. Our reasoning faculty and conscience exist for good reason.

Does it not follow, that every trespasser of natural law self-confesses his/her transgression, simply by his or her action? Natural laws never command, neither is there any need to, yet at once they may reprimand or insist correction and remediation, including possible recompense.

Never did I suspect that natural laws within us, would virtually write a code of rational ethics, in and of themselves.

In the next few chapters, twenty natural laws are listed sequentially, from material existence to natural justice, but they are all interconnected. Each description is brief necessarily, and subsets may append in some cases. Please remember, that natural laws emanate from within the mind and soul of each man and woman as Creator endowed. They cannot be statute written for others to obey. Here, then, are the primary natural laws.

11

NATURAL LAWS 1 TO 5

1 Natural Law of Identity

A thing is what it is and that as the thing is, it acts; conversely as the thing acts, it is.

Nature's Source:

Except for (chosen) actions, there are no facts of random occurrence, such as that could have been different, as against facts that must be. An entity's very own nature determines what it can do, and, dictates what it will do for any given set of circumstances. This natural law exhibits within every man, woman, and child, within every single tissue, cell, organ, system, and faculty of Mans physical, mental, and spiritual being. Man's life is a process of self-sustaining action.

As life progressively enacts, so it exhibits an identity. It is, what we choose that it be. We are its author, and the bearer of its consequential identity.

Ethical and Moral Factors:

Altogether, the sequential orderly relationship that exhibits within Man, that of existence, identity, and conscious identification, is of inestimable importance. Identity is the core tenet of an objective ethical morality. Whatsoever has no identity, cannot be consciously identified. It has no valid ethical or moral import. Devoid of any life-value, nothing of worth offers.

Thus we are prompted to identify the real nature of our self, the true identity of what life is, so to identify what life ought to enact. An objective, ethical morality, is purposefully based on life itself. All pretence is invalid. To change oneself, or the world, one must act according to the reality of their nature, else choices and actions are flawed before they begin. Founding premises are that— Existence exists, Man exists, Man has an identity, a nature, and all are knowable.

Societal application:

Ideas not derived from reality, or evidenced therein, cannot be consistently practised without negative consequence. Man gains no material or spiritual benefit from whims, fancies, or ideologies having no life-upholding foundation. Neither can a society. The Natural Law of Identity applies to the nature of Man himself, to our every thought, consideration, personal interaction with others, politic, and society, and to every business contract and dealing. Refer also the *Natural Law of Causality* and its societal applicability.

> Chapter 22 Reference: The 'Preamble,' and Article 1.3.2, Right to Liberty

2 Natural Law of Causality

> *All action is caused and determined by the nature of the entities that act; no real entity (thing) can occur by chance, or without cause; a thing cannot act contrary to its nature.*

Nature's Source:

This law is innate within Man, exactly as described for the *Natural Law of Identity* (above). The *Law of Causality* is the inevitable consequence of the *Law of Identity*. No real entity (thing) can occur by chance, or without cause. The nature of an action is caused and determined by the nature of the entities that act. Differently stated, a thing cannot act contrary to its nature.

Ethical and Moral Factors:

One may choose to be respected for their actions or disrespected, held in high regard or contempt, blamed or praised, rewarded or penalised, be exonerated, or suffer remediation and (or) recompense penalties.

The two laws of *existence,* and *identity,* must exist before Mans consciousness can identify that which exists. The process of thinking, and the contents of one's thoughts, are two separate things. Efficacy of Mans mind depends entirely on existent reality, the laws of *Identity,* and *Causality,* his discovery and use of them.

Some will argue that nothing is objective, nonetheless the laws of *identity,* and *causality,* are fundamental. They are not rationally deniable. Any attempt to deny these laws will confront the *law of identity.* S/he must be who s/he is—not someone else. The *law of identity* forbids other. Discovered by Aristotle, this law is often called *'reaffirmation through denial.'*

Societal application:

Because a thing cannot act contrary to its nature, (the corollary law of non-contradiction), one's moral nature is revealed by the committed action, not by its ethical, or unethical intent. Responsibility lies with the actor. Restoration of the natural order, i.e. *natural justice,* will focus on restoration, remediation, and recompense, concerning an action, not on apportioning blame. Action and consequence, are the focus of natural justice, not the perpetrator's intention.

The *laws of identity* and *causality* apply to personal ethics, and most especially to the natural law of Justice.

Chapter 22 Reference: Article 1.3.3 - Right to liberty.

3 Natural Law of Independence

All men and women are unique and independent, according to their nature of equally being Man, qua Man.

Nature's Source:

It should be self-evident, and beyond question, that each one of us is an independent element of the human species. Each one by nature is capable of doing, thinking, and saying things, independently of what others are doing, thinking, and saying at the same time. This independence marks each one of us as a separate living being, yet by the nature of being Man, qua (as of) Man, all are equal.

Man's life, his every breath and heart beat, is witness and testament to his (individual) being, without which he cannot exist. The natural laws, (or order) of one's nature, govern every single body function. Mans mind is an attribute of each person, and so is every thought. Man's mental, subconscious, and emotional methods are equal in all respects, but their content is uniquely independent. All body and spirit functions are private in their source. They can be shared, as experiences of life and value exchange, but their source is always individual; inviolate in nature, belonging to each alone. These laws, inherent in every individual man and woman's being, are immutable. They cannot be erased, save by death.

Ethical and Moral Factors:

The separateness of human beings is the natural law of the world. This law is fundamental to our biology, psychology, and praxeology; to our lives, thoughts, feelings, and actions.

Societal application:

Independence, and one's unalienable right to life, are inseparable. Societal dealings should uphold and protect both.

> Chapter 22 Reference: Constitution of Man. Article 1.2 Right of Equality and Sovereignty.

4 Natural Law of Equality

> *All living beings of the Homo sapiens species, are alike nature and faculties, equally endowed.*

Nature's Source:

This law is exhibited by every single tissue, cell, organ, system and faculty of Mans physical, mental and spiritual being without exception, yet every constituent is uniquely different. Each function according to their respective nature, and although processes occur sequentially, not one element of any process is hierarchically superior, more dominating, or authoritative. All support life equally.

Ethical and Moral Factors:

Everyone is equal in possessing the fact of uniqueness, notwithstanding its individualised expression. Appearances and traits will materially differ, but the property by which they are unique remains equal in *concept*. Differentiating characteristics, that define individual uniqueness, serve not to diminish equality, but to emphasise its broad compass, including the individuated faculty of free mind common to all. This union of individual faculty with unique free expression, testifies that all living beings are equal in kind, yet all are enabled independent, separate one from another, in body, mind, and soul.

Societal application:

Without equality, and independence, one's right to life and property, freedom, and convivial society have no meaning.

The union of a particular faculty (one process), testifying equality, with certain free expression (independent content), should properly be the core of Mans business and societal structures; taught in all curricular, from infancy.

> Chapter 22 Reference: Article 1.2 Right of Equality and Sovereignty.

5 Natural Law of Integrity

> *The state of being whole, undivided, integrated, ethically intentioned, and committed to one's life, fully accords with the natural laws of one's nature.*

Nature's Source:

Integrity manifests within Man, as the truthful, honest, holistic cohesiveness of every physical, mental, emotional, and spiritual faculty. Integrity's founding premise is spiritual, namely the upholding of Mans life. Integrity is his core value, the sum of every derivative value, desire, and spiritual goal supporting the totality of life itself. Integrity underscores the whole of Mans physical, conscious, subconscious, emotional and spiritual being.

Ethical and Moral Factors:

Integrity's indubitable resounding success within Man's being, fully endorses proper embrace of the same ethic in all personal and societal intentions, actions, and goals. Lack of integrity results in diminished quality of life, in some form, and to some degree. (Refer to the *law of Just Consequence*.)

Societal application:

Integrity, is the core essence of *respect for the lives of others*. It is the fundamental tenet of all personal, social, business and contractual dealings and should be taught across all curricular.

Chapter 22 Reference: Declaration of Individual Rights. Articles 1.1 to 1.8 inclusive.

12

NATURAL LAWS 6 TO 10

6 Natural Law of Individual Rights

Every man, woman, and child is an independent living being, having individual, immutable, and unalienable right to his or her life, free and independent from any usurpation, or violation, whatsoever

Nature's Source:

Independent Life. One cannot live, without performing the self-sustaining actions of living, or without the right to act in support of their life.

Ethical and Moral Factors:

Individual *right to life,* and its sustenance, is unalienable, immutable and inviolate.

Man's right to the fruits of his labour are inalienable, and inviolate.

Societal application:

- Unalienable right, is Man's right to action; to live and sustain his life, within the rights of all others.

- Inalienable right, is Man's right to the product of his action(s); the right of entitlement (or belonging) to that which his efforts have produced, including improvements and cultivations made to land.
- Man's body, his thoughts, actions, and emotions, are his individually; this true for all others equally.
- Individual Rights, are moral principles that restrain society members from interfering with another's actions.
- Rights belong only to individuals, to every him, and every her, singularly. No collective rights can exist.
- Individual rights impose no obligations on one's neighbours, except to abstain from violating his or her rights.
- Individual Rights of Man preside over all other life forms.

The *Natural Law of Individual Rights* pertains to every unique living (human) being, every politic and society, all personal, business, and societal dealings with others. The above principles should be instituted, and taught, as per the *Constitution of Man*.

Chapter 22 Reference: Article 1.1, Right to Life — Clauses 1.1.1 to 1.1.5 inclusive.

7 Natural Law of Free Will

Free choice of thought and action, by any and all Living Being's, are guaranteed inclusive of the responsibility, liability, and accountability, naturally and inherently flowing therefrom.

Nature's Source:

Mans volitional, cognitive consciousness, is his free will—his tool of survival. Free will is inviolate, testified by the fact that subconscious mind protects Mans cognitive free will.

Ethical and Moral Factors:

Free will thought, guaranteed by Mans nature, requires that its content be willed. Individual choices fuel the database of one's subconscious mind, in turn, sourcing conscience, and emotions. Without free will, no mental, emotional, and spiritual growth is possible. Man is the author of his life.

The word free, means free. There are no exceptions, escape routes, let-outs, excuses, or pardons for refusing to exercise free will, and none for overruling it. No one is commanded to use free will, even by Creator, else there is no free will! Consequences are inescapable notwithstanding. No Man-made construct overruling Man's responsibility to choose, can be permitted. (Witness decisions given in the Nuremberg Trials.)

Free will imparts, and embraces the essence, and vitality, of every natural law herein described. Those who claim free license to overrule free will, regardless of asserted authority, mastery, or divinity, are imposters, renegades, pirates, or psychopaths. Their claims are false, without merit, value, or substance! Free will is unimpeachable, and indestructible. Nothing is enabled to override free consent, save through torture, or traumas that violently and criminally force *submission*; not *agreement*! Because consent may be obtained, by surreptitious means without the victim knowing; e.g. through propaganda or misguided ideology, for example, mental vigilance is essential, per the *natural laws of identity and causality*.

Societal application:

One's free will to think, imparts full responsibility for one's actions, which infers that this law is inherent within one's individual right to act, and bear the consequences. Individual rights, free will, respect, and responsibility, are inseparable. They must be upheld and protected, as shown in the *Constitution of Man*, and the *Commission of Justice* at www.naturalelaw.com

Chapter 22 Reference: The Preamble, plus Articles 1.1 to 1.5 inclusive. Additionally, Article 1.5 Right of abdication, Clause 1.5.1, and 1.6, Right of Independence, Clause 1.6.1

8 Natural Law of Commitment

To live is to commit to actions and bear the consequences.

Nature's Source:

Man's Nature. Mans volitional consciousness enables free choice, including the commitment to act, necessarily bearing the consequences of one's actions. Mans nature offers no automated alternative, as for other life forms.

Ethical and Moral Factors:

Free will is the committed intention to exercise one's free choice, to achieve a particular outcome, or result from a chosen action, and to bear responsibility for that action. Every man, and woman, authors the consequences of his or her efforts, regardless of what thought evaluation prompted it, (mitigating circumstances accepted). Moral responsibility, and accountability, are expressed by the action. (Refer to the *Natural Law of Just Consequence*.)

Societal application:

This law falls squarely within all personal, social and business dealings, and the jurisdiction of natural justice.

Chapter 22 Reference: Article 1.3 Right to Liberty, clauses 1.3.1 and 1.3.2

9 Natural Law of Allowance

Every man, woman, and child (including infants and those mentally handicapped) are endowed to venture, to progress at their choice and pace, in service of their life, but are not absolved from refusing, so to do.

Nature's Source:

Creator has endowed, that Mans subconscious mind may fully function, including for emotions, even although the cognitive mind is unable, but not unwilling, to perform at its fullest potential.

Ethical and Moral Factors:

Infants, young children, and those who suffer from a mental handicap, are enabled to choose their actions, and experience the emotions of success, or failure, while they progressively grow as best possible, in cognitive mental stature, understanding, and spirituality. This law allows for lessons of support, and correction, and for those teachings to be consciously woven into the tapestry of one's conscious, and subconscious minds, by one's free will choice, thereby facilitating and stimulating mental growth, and development as one chooses.

This Law accommodates maturity, as its student learns to master his or her fulfillments in life. It permits learning, and spiritual maturity, to become habituated throughout one's entire adult life. That is its purpose and function. It is the window through which habituation of the learning process, enables consistently higher percentiles of truth to amass in one's intuit database, in turn fostering greater reliability, and certainty, with least effort. (See the *Natural Law of Efficacy*)

Societal application:

This law applies to every living being of human species. Ethically, morally, and spiritually, it endorses that one recognise and accept others rights, and ability to progress at their pace, according to their choices and abilities. This law should underscore all personal, educational, business, and societal dealings with others. It is the foundation stone of all education, cooperation, and collaboration; relationships, marriage, and parenthood included.

It has particular relevance to schooling at all levels, including for adult education. Devotees and students of Steiner, and Montessori education, will recognise its potency in a flash! This *Natural Law of Allowance* speaks of graciousness, politeness, integrity, gratitude, and respect. It facilitates the development of mental competence, consistent with choice yet without penalty. It facilitates ever increasing mental efficiency, over time, that makes clear that mental and emotional development, is the requirement of a full and prosperous life. No (purported) Law, that Man has ever invented, can match Creator's achievement that this natural law allows, and never will it. Man's laws can only trespass it.

> Chapter 22 Reference: Article 1.3 Right to Liberty, Clauses 1.3.2 and 1.3.3

(Abuse of the Law of Allowance)

Abuse of this law occurs far too often, yet its victims, who mostly believe they've suffered an unfortunate consequence, rarely understand that indeed they caused it. Mental abstention resulting from apathy, indifference, or lazy refusal to exercise one's mental faculties, is not an impaired or debilitated faculty. No excuse is permitted, and no allowance is made, for *choosing* to be mentally vacant, deprived, or retarded. Harmful consequences that may result, are of one's free choice in such cases, as justly they deserve to be.

The *Law of Allowance* does not, and cannot compel self-initiated development, for that would trespass free will. Instead, it justly allows the *full consequences* of one's choices for better or worse, this being the *Natural Law of Just Consequence*.

Societal application:

Abuse of this law falls within the jurisdiction of natural justice.

> Chapter 22 Reference: Article 1.3 Right to Liberty, Clauses 1.3.2 and Article 1.5 Right of Abdication Clause 1.5.3

10 Natural Law of Respect

No man, woman, or child can uphold their unalienable right to life without correspondingly respecting the equal right to life, of all other living human beings.

Nature's Source:

Every constituent, organ, system, process, and faculty of Man, exists to support life, each entity having its own nature. Independent in function, yet united in purpose, each fully respects the individual success of all other supportive entities, regardless of uniqueness, difference, or diversity, else its own function and life is compromised, or snuffed out.

Ethical and Moral Factors:

We respect our bodies by eating nutritious foods, exercising, sleeping, and cleansing; our minds by practising thought, and our hearts by relaxation, and meditation. We respect things of beauty, by travel, by visiting galleries, or revelling in the great outdoors. We respect our efforts by properly preparing, ordering, and doing. Our life entirely depends on self-respect, for natural order, and natural laws within ourselves.

The lesson begins at home, from an ethical standpoint. It encompasses all aspects of our lives, and our chosen values. These include respect for thinking, identity and causality, right reason, investigation, truthfulness, values, conscience, emotions, thoughtfulness, actions, consequences, and the lives of others. Unrelenting respect, for the free life of others, is the only guarantee of our freedom, period! In short, self-respect, and respect for others, should be one's core principle in life, physiologically, psychologically, emotionally and spiritually.

Societal application:

Respect manifests through moral, or immoral actions, to become the primary factor in all matters concerning *natural justice*. Respect, is exhibited by those who uphold the natural law, rejected conversely, by all those who trespass. Respect, and its relationship to natural justice, should be the core ethic taught in all curricular, from infancy onwards.

Respect for self, and all others, necessitates that Individual Rights be instituted, then protected from all trespass and violation, as described in the *Constitution of Man*. Whosoever disagrees this fundamental fact of life, should take their petition to Mans Creator, not to an (irrelevant) court of legal jurisdiction.

Constitution of Man Reference: The entire document.

13

NATURAL LAWS 11 TO 15

11 Natural Law of Reciprocity

Respect for one's individual life, and reciprocally for the right of all others to live, guarantees the freedom, and right of all others of the human species.

Nature's Source:

Every constituent, and faculty of Mans physical, mental, and spiritual being, uphold the common purpose of life, yet all are uniquely different, and independent. It cannot be otherwise, since their aggregate success guarantees continuance, and maintenance of the (societal) environment in which each singularly prospers. (Refer also to the *Law of No Trespass*.)

Ethical and Moral Factors:

Moral discipline asserts, that where the rights of all other individuals are respected, no one can offend another by any application of his, or her own. Freedom to live by one's nature and personal choices, applies to all of us, or it is not freedom at all. All contrary claims are anti-life. Any quarrel is with Creator, and none other.

Societal application:

This law applies to every unique living being—every politic, and society. Institution of this law, necessarily cancels every Man-made statute, or directive, that violates Creator's invitation to live.

Creator has ruled, that one's independent life is conditional upon the maintenance of a societal environment guaranteeing that each life may prosper. This natural law, does not ensure that each will prosper, for that is the prerogative of free will. Instead, it maintains an environment that permits each one to thrive. It is for Man, to translate this law into a free convivial society, upholding reciprocal individual rights to life, property, and freedom.

> Chapter 22 Reference: Constitution of Man. Article 1.2 Right of Equality and Sovereignty.

12 Natural Law of Right Reason

Reasoning discovers truths that are not self-evident—to adapt material existence to life-sustaining purposes.

Nature's Source:

Nature of Man. Volitional consciousness. *Reasoning* is the intellectual ability to logically think through connected steps, in search of truths that are not self-evident. It is the mental means by which rational beings understand themselves, think about cause and effect, truth and falsehood, ethics and morality.

Ethical and Moral Factors:

A science of ethics, later discussed, entirely depends on the use of volitional consciousness. Reason, facilitates an ability to change attitudes, traditions, and institutions, and to convert beliefs into knowledge, within the realm of free will, and self-determination.

Societal application:

This Law properly applies to every unique living being, every politic, and society.

> Chapter 22 Reference: Article 1.2 Right of Equality and Sovereignty. Article 1.3 Right to Liberty, Clause 1.3.2. Article 1.6 Right of Independence Clauses 1.6.1 and 1.6.2 11 Natural Law of Reciprocity

13 Natural Law of Efficacy

Related conscious faculties, permit efficacious functioning, correspondent with valid and truthful mental content.

Nature's Source:

Man's faculty of perception, testifies automatic integration of vast amounts of raw, truthful, uncorrupted data. Cognitive mind's (word) concept vocabulary, also integrates a multiplicity of data, for fast and efficient mental functioning. However, because free will is involved, this data may be true, misleading, or false. Efficient mental functioning is handicapped, when data is corrupted.

Emotional feelings derive, in part, from consciously implanted, or subconsciously assimilated values, any of which may be true, misleading, or false. Efficacy is assisted, or harmed.

Ethical and Moral Factors:

Efficacy of thought and reasoning, efficiency, accurate and speedy resolutions, intuition, life-values, and emotional stability, are all affected according to whether mental data that we process is truthful, or corrupted. The *Natural Law of Efficacy* enables one who places a high value on mental agility, truth, validity, and integrity, to speed past those who must mentally wrestle every issue, with a high degree of certainty and truth.

Societal application:

This law, upholds all other natural laws without exception. It teaches that all erroneous beliefs, fictional laws, mysticism, subjectivism, perverted meanings, including misconstructions of language and stolen concepts, will deprive, or mislead cognitive understanding; hinder or cripple cognitive comprehension. This law applies materially, mentally, emotionally, and spiritually, to every aspect of self, every goal, and ambition. Every desire to simplify and expedite the demands, and desires of life is amplified. Emotional deprivations and traumas minimise, while boundless joy maximises. This law applies to every element of education, every politic, and society, and every personal, business and societal dealing with others.

> Chapter 22 Reference: This law is so overwhelmingly pertinent to Mans efficacious wellbeing, life, and spiritual essence, that every clause in the *Constitution of Man* upholds it.

14 Natural Law of Ethics

> *Ethics, is the science of choosing life-supporting thoughts, values, and determinations, that when acted upon, outwardly express an individual's morality.*

Nature's Source:

Man's physical, intellectual, and spiritual nature. Man is by nature obliged to adapt material reality to his purposes, inviting ethical, life-sustaining thinking and reasoning to found his actions.

Ethical and Moral Factors:

Ethics [plural] is a free will chosen *code of principles* that govern the moral correctness of an individuals behaviour, actions and activities. Ethics embrace wholesome integrity, testifying the truthful, honest, wholesome cohesiveness of Man's every physical mental, emotional and spiritual faculty.

Ethics impel but cannot ever compel, that every man and woman think and act in a manner supportive of life. Consistent assessment and appraisal of values respectful of one's life, should properly implant life sustaining 'ethics' in subconscious mind, so as to monitor and uphold moral actions.

Societal application:

Ethics, as a chosen code of principles governing correctness, resides within one's thoughts, within one's mind. No other individual is affected by one's self-contained ethics. Unethical thinking and reasoning occasions no harm to anyone but oneself, including emotional consequences. A science of ethics (from its source perspective) should be inclusive within all education curricula across all levels of education.

Resultant actions let the ethical cat out of the bag. Morality is expressed by actions, that are moral, amoral, or immoral. These may indeed affect others, for which one is wholly accountable and responsible. Immoral actions may occasion harm to self and others. (Refer to the Natural Law of No Trespass, and the Natural Law of Just Consequence.)

> Chapter 22 Reference: |Declaration of Individual Rights, Articles 1.1 to 1.4 inclusive. Additionally, Article 1.6 Right of Independence Clauses 1.6.1 and 1.6.2

15 Natural Law of Morality

Actions, and behaviour, publicly testify one's pre-conceived moral stature, and agreed moral accountability.

Nature's Source:

Every cell, tissue, organ, system and function of our body, and every mental process (not content), is tasked, to uphold every other constituent of our life. Their every purpose, their reason, their collaboration, and full accountability, is their moral stature. Life could not exist otherwise.

Ethical and Moral Factors:

Is it not self-evident, that Man should always act in full support of his own life? Should Man embrace moral integrity, and spiritual uprightness, of will and character, also granting that his fellows may do the same? What else requires explanation? Morality is of each independent living being, who, therefore, is accountable for its manifestation or lack. Morality is not a social edict. This law applies to all of Mans actions, and behaviours, and all accountability arising from there. *Natural justice*, is its adjudicator.

Societal application:

Man's nature testifies that immoral action, being a violation of another's right to life, does not break natural law—it reinforces and amplifies its necessity. It cogently points, to necessary correction.

Immoral action, once proven, is the perpetrators self-confessed trespass of natural law; their self-admitted guilt. Their actions confirm their agreement to bear natural justice, as a self-confessed *outlaw*. Outlaws are not free. They have consciously chosen, to surrender their freedom by their immoral and /or unlawful actions, or behaviour. (Refer to the *Law of Natural Justice*.)

> Chapter 22 Reference: Declaration of Individual Rights, Articles 1.1 to 1.5 inclusive; all clauses pertaining to actions.

14

NATURAL LAWS 16 TO 20

16 Natural Law of Cooperative Enterprise

Cooperative effort with others, will return more benefit than most individual's can achieve alone.

Nature's Source:

Man's nature testifies the synergistic effort of every individual constituent, collaboratively working with all others. No dispute or conflict exists. Conscience, emotions, and the immune system, serve to remedy divergence from the goal of living, to ameliorate, or cure discord, trauma, and disease. Likewise, conscious mind, and subconscious mind, work cooperatively to mutual benefit.

Ethical and Moral Factors:

Exactly as body cells, systems, and faculties are not permitted to trespass upon another, so as to violate their function, so they are correspondingly endowed to co-operate for synergistic benefit. Cooperative, collaborative enterprise satisfies the *natural law of no trespass,* in all respects, while upholding the *laws of equality, independence, right reason, efficacy and morality.*

Societal application:

Cooperative enterprise, means that individuals are the source of purposive actions, that requires that their individual rights prevail, over any societal or business structure they may have instituted. Group rights, are thereby ousted, eminent domain also. Business, and contractual dealings, found on the same principles of independence, voluntary cooperation, and one's unalienable right to life.

> Chapter 22 Reference: Declaration of Individual Rights, Articles 1.1 to 1.9 inclusive, and very specifically Article 1.5, Right of Abdication, Clauses 1.5.1 and 1.5.2

17 Natural Law of No Trespass

> *No independent living being has the right to trespass, or to violate another's life, or property.*

Nature's Source:

Creator has endowed, that no constituent of Man including his body cells, systems, and faculties, are enabled to trespass on another, such as would hinder or harm function. The subconscious mind is forbidden to overrule conscious mind, and vice versa. Free will has absolute autonomy; free of any and all trespass, no matter by whom, or by what. Nothing may violate, or infringe natural process.

Ethical and Moral Factors:

This law simply and directly translates, to absolutely *No Trespass,* of any other living being's right to life. Notice that *respect for all others,* and *no violation of the rights of others,* are tantamount to being identical.

Societal application:

Two persons cannot be free and equal, when one of them is controlling, managing, threatening, blackmailing, or extorting the other.

- Man's right to act, so to live, fully accepts the reciprocal right of all others, equally so to do.
- Trespass of another's rights, self-cancel one's personal rights, respective of any relevant action.
- No claim of right, may negate, usurp, or overrule the unalienable rights of other living human beings.
- Independent rights of Man, preside over all other life forms.

No form of eminent domain, shall henceforth exist. *(Eminent domain' means resumption/compulsory acquisition, or expropriation; e.g. the power of a state or a national government to take private property for public use.)* Respective of one's right to independent life, that is trespass.

The *Constitution of Man* upholds this law in full, while the *Commission of Justice* is tasked with preserving it.

Chapter 22 Reference: Article 1, Declaration of Individual Rights, and Article 2. Group Rights; all clauses inclusive.

18 Natural Law of Just Consequence

Nature serves just consequence, whether respected or not.

Nature's Source:

All actions have consequences. Aside from natural causes, commonly referred to as Acts of God, all actions result from one's ethical choices. Man is the author, and practitioner of his actions, just recipient of their consequences thereby.

The *Law of Just Consequence,* justly allows the full consequences of one's choices, for better or worse. Whereas the *Law of Allowance* applies to alleviate, or overcome legitimate impairment of some kind, the *Law of Just Consequence* precludes its abuse. No excuses apply, save mitigating circumstances.

Ethical and Moral Factors:

This law mimics Francis Bacon's statement, *'Nature to be commanded must be obeyed.'* Given free will, the word *respect,* is more accurate than the word *obey.*

Just consequence does not necessarily mean that a consequence will be the exact measure of an action's morality, or immorality, although this will be true more often than not. Efforts jointly contributed by others, or mitigating circumstances may apply. *Just consequence* means it justly belongs; belongs *exactly* to whoever caused it.

The *Natural Law of Just Consequence,* is the essence of *natural justice.* It permits *exactly* what one chooses, whether for good or evil, and it makes no mistakes. See Chapter 19.

Mans moral obligation to himself, is to learn of this law, and learn from it. It is the core of Mans conscience, and emotions, not forgetting bodily dis-ease.

Societal application:

This law, applies to every unique living (human) being, every politic, and society. It is a core tenet of the science of ethics, and foundation of the *Natural Law of Justice.*

Chapter 22 Reference: The Constitution of Man, Article 1.5.1.

19 Natural law of Forceful Arrest

Arrest of all initiated force, protects Man's unalienable right to life.

Nature's Source:

Every element, and aspect of Man's nature, prove Creator's endowment of this law and its vital necessity. The *Laws of Just Allowance, Morality, No Trespass, Just Consequence, and Natural Justice,* are further witness. As Mans nature testifies in total, all initiated coercive, or physical force, all acts of aggression, violate one's free will, and one's right to life.

Ethical and Moral Factors:

Supreme mental coercion, e.g., fraud and blackmail, that deny Mans perception of reality, or threat of physical destruction that forces him to act against his judgment, negates, and paralyses his means of survival.

Whoever initiates the use of force, for whatever purpose, to whatever extent, is a killer, intent on destroying Man's capacity to live! Force, and mind, are opposites. To herd, and rule men and women, those who invent *legalities* define their individual character correspondingly. They cannot claim the sanction of reason, as no advocate of contradictions can claim it.

Societal application:

Without protection, or self defence, Man is at the mercy of all who initiate force, including governments, fraudsters, blackmailers, tyrants, rapists, psychopaths, terrorists, thugs, war mongers and murderers.

The precondition of a civilised society, is the barring of physical force from social relationships. Nature has established the principle, that if men and women wish to deal with one another, they may do so only by reason, by discussion, persuasion, and voluntary, uncoerced agreement. (Refer to the *Natural Law of Cooperative Enterprise*.)

Security of each person, and his or her property against predatory attack, emerges as a most necessary condition of society. Protection of Individual Rights is the function of the *Commission of Justice*. (see http://naturalelaw.com)

> Chapter 22 Reference: Declaration of Individual Rights; Article 1.7, Right of Protection — both clauses.

20 Natural Law of Justice

> *Innocent, natural individuals are free. Proven trespassers of natural law, are outlaws, perpetrators of deliberately enacted transgressions, voluntary bearers of natural justice.*

Nature's Source:

Creator has modelled the principle of *natural justice*, right in the core of one's conscience, and emotional reporting systems, exactly where it belongs. Conscience, and emotions, inform of justice or injustice—what is upholding one's life, or hindering it.

Ethical and Moral Factors:

Every individual is author of their own internalised, thought-based ethics. Their actions, translate directly into moral justness, or immoral unjustness, served upon others.

Those, who (secretly) self-declare that others can be walked over, trodden on, and their rights ground into dust, have inwardly rejected morality. Correspondingly their actions will outwardly broadcast they are in need of *restorative justice*; needing to be returned to a state of natural order and its natural laws.

Free persons do not commit crimes—those who have (prior) chosen, to relinquish their freedom, do. The full force of *Natural Justice* is brought to bear upon such perpetrators, being the only force he, or she, has the right to choose. *Lawful remediation* is now the path of *natural justice*. No legal instrument may preside contrary; all such are unjust and unlawful.

Societal application:

A full expose of Natural Justice follows in Chapter 19.

> Chapter 22 Reference: Articles 3, 4, 5 and 6; Declaration of Individual Rights, Article 1.5; Right of Abdication, Clauses 1.5.1, and 1.5.2

15

MORAL SOCIETY

Society

The word *society* has several meanings. For most people, it means community, the public, the people, the population, the world, humankind, mankind, the human species. From the standpoint of culture, it means a group, community, civilisation, or nation. Others use the word to mean a form of high society, aristocracy, the gentry, the nobility, the upper classes, the elite, or privileged classes. Others will consider it refers to a body, a guild, college, lodge, order, fraternity, brother or sisterhood, sorority, federation, union, alliance, or institution. Last, but not least, from the perspective of shared company, it means companionship, fellowship, friendship, comradeship, camaraderie, and social intercourse.

That almost inexhaustible list, effectively amounts to the word *society* having no definitive meaning at all. Two outcomes are possible. First, it enables all of us to comfortably feel that we share in a broad community, that we belong to a group, and are not an *outsider*. Second, it's all-encompassing nature never begs we ask exactly what society is. Of relevance here, is that it never prompts us to discover the relationship of government to society.

That government claims to act in the interests of *society* is comforting to most folk. They welcome cultural association, contributing to society, to availing themselves of government protections, and benefits. They perceive society as something that binds us all together as a people, and as a country, or nation. So they are lulled into accepting the word *society*, because it comfortably embraces the cohesive totality of their life.

Sadly, indeed tragically, that description hides proper understanding of what society is, from its political perspective.

What is society? (*societas, ibi ius*) The answer, depends on what type of society the question refers. Fundamentally there are two kinds, or are interpreted in two ways—

- Societas in the *exclusive sense*—this being *society as company,* usually what we refer to as government, but also with other reference.
- Or, in the *inclusive sense*—where the word *society* refers to *society-as-symbiosis*. This describes interaction between two different organisms, living in close physical association, typically to the advantage of both.

Conditions of, and for the existence of both, differ widely.

Society as Company: (Social Rules)

Society as Company, applies to all social systems governed by a system of invented rules. These include sporting clubs, charitable and educational institutions, corporations, and governments, that today are corporations. Although we commonly consider society, as an aggregation of people living and freely interacting with one another in an atmosphere of liberty, strictly speaking, that is very seldom correct. Tribes, far removed from what we think of as a society, may indeed be socially acclimated, yet fully free as individuals.

Converse to tribal freedom, and free association, *exclusive societies* such as clubs, institutions, corporations, and corporate government, rely on, and demand, that their subjects give *exclusive* attention to its societal self, and its nature, especially to its preservation. Thus we all are bound to its social rules. *Rule-bound company,* is what the word *society* means. Loyalty to its members and leaders is foremost. Members, constituents, and its citizens, highly prize fairness of its governance; its government. All consider themselves beneficiaries.

Society by company, is primarily concerned with relationships, between its constituent parts and its organised whole, in the context of its, sometimes but not always disclosed, purposeful existence. What members, or citizens do, and how, is more fundamental, essential to the society, to its office bearers, managers, CEO's, and employees, than to those it serves.

Rules, governing the management of these societies, are not law within their original meaning, neither a science. Instead, they are *artificial orders, of artificial persons*, who's *legal systems* must attach legal rights, duties, and obligations, to its *organisational positions*.

Artificial order, is an order of *artificial persons*. Artificial persons are not living human beings. They are positions, roles or functions within a particular game, social system or society, governed by a system of (invented) rules, that facilitate their (respective) functioning. Think of artificial persons, for example, as white and black pieces in a game of chess, including the particular governing rules of the King, Queen, Knights, Pawns, etcetera. Other examples include such as Rector, Dean, Student or Faculty member in a university, or King, Government, Parliament, Minister and Citizen in a nation-state.

Such legal artifice, *does not attach to the actual living beings,* elected or appointed to occupy those positions. Indeed, this legal separation, removes any misdeeds or personal liability from public accountability. It excuses, and exonerates those who serve those organisational roles, save for censure(s) within the company itself.

E.g. Susan didn't do it, the *branch manager* did. No living individual is legally accountable; only the *position*. Notice how every government document is signed off, by an office bearer.

Society as Company: (Government) Positive law

As above, *Law,* in today's world is called *Positive Law, or Legal Positivism,* common law included. It is Man-made, *statute law.*

To make rules for the managing of government, the word *person*, that we all think means you and me, has been usurped, and construed to have a legal meaning. Your natural (flesh and blood) nature, legally stolen from you at birth, has a body politic attached. The word person now describes a fictional, a LEGAL ENTITY having legal obligations, within the *society by company.*

Usurping your born name, government's have you believe that your legal entity is the real you. Passport's, driver's licence's, and ID cards, are your legal ID, so you're told, but they are not your ID. Those instruments are *their ID.* They identify the legal entity that is government's corporate slave. So it is that you are recognised only as that LEGAL ENTITY, a *citizen* by NAME, subservient to the (legal) *(society by company)* government, to be ruled and regulated, as a servant slave, all taught as for your benefit. Every time you show *their ID* upon request, fully believing it is your ID, *you agree to be their servant.* So they claim *consent of the governed.*

Little known, we are also commanded by statutes, and directives, and coerced by propaganda and misleading practices, including by the legal profession, into believing that natural flesh and blood living beings are *natural persons.* Yet, unbeknown to almost everyone, *natural persons* are legally deemed to be *Legal Entities.* Thus *natural persons* are not living human beings, legally. So it is that we all act for, and as the *legal entity;* our individual rights trampled as though they never existed. Natural law rejected—statute laws reign supreme—backed by deadly force.

You have no natural born rights, today, as a (flesh and blood) breathing individual. Nonetheless, government entirely depends on your flesh and blood body, participating as, and acting in the capacity of the (fictional) legal entity, known by your *citizen* NAME, as though you really were it.

All such *citizens* are dead, however. Legal entities are fictional inventions. Your NAME is a fiction. Constitutional usurpation of your born name, the process that makes it your LEGAL NAME, is a fraud. All fraud is void-abinitio, meaning from the beginning. It cannot be amended or fixed. Abandonment, it's only absolution.

> We are fast approaching the stage of the ultimate inversion: the stage where the government is free to do anything it pleases, while the citizens may act only by permission; which is the stage of the darkest periods of human history, the stage of rule by brute force. —Ayn Rand (written 60 years ago)

Most people have no idea that we function, in *positive law*, as and for a counterfeit legal entity, stolen from our born name without our consent. Most people live in complete ignorance of this deception. Had they given consent, they would have known. Through ignorance, they support *consent of the governed,* to the utter delight of those who rule us.

Common Law, ostensibly overturns this misappropriation, by claiming *natural law* to be its foundation. Notwithstanding that claim, whatsoever purportedly upholds natural law, but fails to reject *rule*, confesses preeminence of *positive law*. Then, sadly, the (natural) moral law is hidden from sight, and understanding, to the point that victims have no knowledge it even exists.

It follows that governments are the (legal) monopolists of terror; the very thing they claim to abhor. Although they state, that their purpose is your protection, your wellbeing is maintained sufficient only for *legal citizens, aka natural persons,* to be their slave labour force. Without, their *society by company*' would collapse.

Should it surprise that very few perceive of any means to overcome legal oppression, slavery, tyranny and unceasing war? So-called leaders know this well. They much prefer that natural laws remain concealed, which describes, why knowledge of full consciousness has been occulted throughout Mans entire history.

Meanwhile, government violence, and coercion, increases in quantity and severity. We vote for its continuance out of ignorance, while government protects your legal status, at all cost, so that their empire survives. Censorship, propaganda, state schooling, licensing, and registration, political correctness, and media control all serve their purpose. Thus structured, and provisioned by your labours, governments have taken unto themselves the right to use force, and coercion, to preserve and protect their *society by company*.

History repeatedly shows the foolish irrationality of majorities, proudly and loudly proclaimed today as *democracy*. The direction such control takes is mostly academic. Corporate political power, is nothing but a state-run monopoly, using methods that enforce its perpetuity, at the expense of the people enslaved to uphold it. The notion that authority is benefactor, and protector, is a monstrous lie. It is impossible! No truly moral, honest, individual man or woman, can participate or endorse the (initiated) coercing of others, for any reason.

Such society, cannot be amended to serve living beings. Man is not his brother's keeper. We are indeed keepers in that we are not to commit acts of violence against one another. We are not keepers in that some must command others, even for their supposed benefit. Authority, backed by force, is an act of violence, antithetical of all benefits it purportedly upholds.

Authority

Corporatised government's criminal success was to replace who, (living) men and women, with what, (non-living) fictional entities, called *natural persons,* or *citizens.* Violation of Mans life is declared to be *legal* therefore, deliberately misconstrued as *lawful,* backed by force, which methodology is taught and upheld as both moral, and just. All is skilfully hidden in plain sight, so that masses approve its perpetuity at the polling booth.

So Man clings to governmental edicts despite sufferance. He does not equate harms, with having forsaken or abused Creator's natural laws, and so will demand more legislative authority enforced by violence, for every failing of government's power. That sums today's world—indeed Man's entire history—mayhem, war, carnage and endless bloodshed its result.

Some seek release, pointing to natural law as the remedy. Not found in the literature, or written in any of Man's law library's, they reach a dead end. Others profess, that no facts connect Mans nature to his legislations. Thus no society is possible outside of Man-made legalities, backed by force. Government is indispensable they conclude; violent anarchy perceived it's only alternative. So they reach a dead end also.

Nothing will change, until Man awakens to this crime against humanity, and utterly eliminates it. Corporatised government, has known from inception, that it could only succeed; first, while its citizens remain ignorant of its (counterfeit) methods, and second, while living men and women have no understanding of their rights, and natural laws endowed by Creator. Government dismissal of what is natural and just, is nothing but a few individuals arrogantly asserting their power to command nature, or dismiss it. By agreement, we sacrifice our endowed nature, to governmental power that (forcibly) commands it.

We do not arrest these tyrants, who fraudulently claim moral status, thus criminality survives by our consent. We are taught to accept, that nothing is humanly possible but statute laws backed by force, demanding our full support at the polling booth. We totally believe the lie. Governments understand our entrapment in full.

Man is obliged to divorce from the dead, fictional LEGAL ENTITY that has usurped his or her name, for example, Joe BLOW, or Mr J Blow, or JOE BLOW and other derivatives. Joe Blow is an independent, flesh and blood, living being, not a LEGAL ENTITY.

Only then, will the criminal enterprise of government, *society by company,* fall flat on its face.

Positive law vs Justice

Natural order, being natural law, is not commandment. Of crucial importance, is that orderliness of process, within Man, his natural laws, have been endowed by Creator to secure life, its comforts, and security. Man's being is complete, in all respects. Not one thing more is needed, given free choice, commitment, and respect for the lives of all others.

Man is thereby enabled with free choice, to grasp and understand his completeness, with its comforts and securities, to determine to adhere them, in a social context that upholds and protects all. Nothing could be more simple. Nothing could better serve justice.

Today's *justice systems* are perceived by almost everyone, to uphold one's rights as a living being. The truth is very different. No reconciliation, or compromise is possible, between real and artificial, now or ever! Meanwhile, incomprehensibly, thousands if not millions, daily fight in courts in every country, attempting to reconcile the *natural law* of living beings, with the *positive law* of *artificial beings,* as though some conciliation, or meeting ground was humanly possible. It's not!

Positive law-courts, bound by the nature and structure of *Society by Company,* must banish natural law as incompatible; because it is. Whatever *natural law* evidence presents in these courts; the presenter is nonetheless held to be *natural person*; an artificial *legal entity,* within a *legal jurisdiction* based on *artificial order.* Who will complain when they have no understanding of this subterfuge? Unknowingly, therefore, *every presenter in today's courts, confesses that artificial order (law) will preside*, simply by presenting to that court's jurisdiction. The court *must dismiss all natural law presentments,* because none accord with its jurisdiction.

Will *Society by Company* ever be done away? Not while it writes the legal, and moral rule book, that enforce compliance with gunpowder laws! Neither will it vanish, while human sciences ignore the natural laws of Mans being as though non-existent. It will remain while Creator's invitation to fully live remains deliberately hidden, by religious, and/or secular contrivance. It will survive while political authority violates Man's right to life, on every continent, endorsed by (polling booth) billions as a just, moral, legal society, offering benefits comforts and security. *Society by Company* will not fade into oblivion while Man disavows his independent being, as Creator endowed, preferring instead to be herded, branded, and corralled as a *social animal.*

The crossroad of consciousness

Enough! Man has reached the crossroads of his consciousness. His ability to identify, and separate fact from fiction, is unequivocal, but what will he do?

If Man is ever to redeem his life from the hock shop of legal criminality, then life is the starting point, the only reference base for all investigations and conclusions, no exceptions. Whoever disagrees, disavows their God-given nature, that automatically rules their protest inadmissible.

Understanding is crucial, if Man is ever to attain the free,, convivial society Creator always intended should be.

16

INDIVIDUAL RIGHTS

Right to life

Man's right to his life, and to uphold it, are existent properties of his individual, independent self. No act, decree, or legislation of Man can alter that fact. The source of *individual rights* is not divine law, or congressional law, but the *Law of Identity*. Each man, and woman, are impelled by nature to sustain his or her life, through his or her effort. If not so chosen, he or she perishes, unless another person steps in to fulfil that function.

The right to life, is not the right to a product, service, result, or outcome, but nature's entitlement to the *actions of living*. Without the right, to act in support of life, it is curtailed, decreased, or deprived. Further, if one's right to life is overruled, or denied, one's life is violated. Thus *individual rights* are conditions of existence, required by every man and woman's nature, for his or her sustenance and survival.

Just as there is no collective lung, heart, brain, or digestive system to be sustained, so there is no *unified life* to be sustained by collective human rights. Individuals may associate, cooperate, and collaborate, but no associative dealing can negate one's free right to life. Every politic and society, should endorse the applicability of individual rights, summarised by this list, and fully enumerated in Chapter 22.

- One cannot rightfully live, without the individual right to act, so to live.
- Whosoever preaches or decrees otherwise, holds death as his or her premise.
- No claim of right, may negate, or usurp, the unalienable rights of any other living human being.
- Man's body, his thoughts, emotions, and actions, are inherently his life—his responsibility, therefore—this reciprocally valid for all others equally.
- No collective rights are possible, without usurping each individual's right to his or her life.
- Individual rights, impose no obligations on one's neighbours, except to abstain from violating his or her rights. Individual rights, guarantee one's freedom to think and act.
- Man's right to act, so to live, cannot exist, or be just, without fully accepting the reciprocal right of all others equally so to do.
- Whereas animals must adapt themselves to nature, and Man must adapt nature to himself, so the individual rights of Man to live, necessarily preside over all other life forms.
- Man has the immutable, unalienable right to live as a rational being, and is impelled by his nature so to do. Nonetheless, Man's free will allows him to think, and act irrationally, immorally and unjustly, recipient of just consequences in like measure. (The *Natural Law of Just Consequence*)

Right to Thoughts vs Right to Actions

Natural rights, are individual rights, necessarily to be protected if Man is to be free.

> A natural right in the strict sense is that which is naturally under a person's control, his body with its faculties of

> movement, feeling, thought, and speech. By extension, a natural right is what a person brings under his control without violating any other person's natural rights. —Frank Van Dun [viii]

Observe the profound accuracy of that statement. The first sentence speaks of ethical consideration. It does not say a natural right is *one's action*. It does not say that one has a natural right to a thing or some outcome, e.g., to an *education* or *health care*. It says a natural right, is (self) control over one's faculties, without violating another's rights.

That explanation, highlights two of the most fundamental facts of human existence, concerning natural law.

- Your right to life, and your freedom, is guaranteed when every other individual's right to their life is upheld. Reciprocal rights, emphatically emphasises need for the institution of individual rights; to preserve, and protect them from ever being repealed, or repudiated.
- Transgressors, who by their immoral and unjust action(s), voluntarily forfeit their freedom, correspondingly admit that restorative natural justice is to be borne by them, according to the measure of their chosen transgression.

That is to say, actions that preserve others rights, guarantee one's own. Conversely, actions that violate others rights, forfeit one's own, and invoke natural justice in like measure. Without, no rights, and no freedoms are possible.

Free will can be abused, plundered, violated, usurped, or negated. Many do. They portend, that free will is the right to do what they prefer, when so chosen, to whomever, regardless of all else, and all consequences. Some claim this right is given by God, hence the Divine Right of Kings. This abomination, has secularly translated into every government that has ever existed, premised on the (self-claimed) right of a few, to rule all others.

Human rights

The Universal Declaration of Human Rights (UDHR), to which Australia is a signatory, was adopted by the United Nations General Assembly, in December 1948, at the Palais de Chaillot, Paris. This document is believed by most people, to enunciate the rights to which all individual human beings are inherently entitled, from which liberty is guaranteed. Does it indeed?

Article 1 states—*'All human beings are born free and equal in dignity and rights.'* As though that clause did not exist, Article 29 (3) states— *'These rights and freedoms may in no case be exercised contrary to the purposes and principles of the United Nations.'*

Even simpletons, should scream indignation to that insanity! Article 29, completely smashes Article 1. Freedom, rights, equality, and dignity, are politically and categorically overruled—no exceptions! Worse even, your born (living) nature, and your right to life, are subject to United Nations permission—all counterclaims denied. You are a chattel, a slave, period!

Does that emphasise, that Man has reached the crossroads of his consciousness—that his task is to identify and separate the facts of his life, and unalienable right to live, from all contemptuous criminal rule in violation thereof? Individual, unalienable rights, are the only key to Man's freedom.

Unalienable Rights

Unalienable rights, and *inalienable* rights, are considered by many people to mean the same thing. This confusion, seemingly arises from the words Latin and French roots, referencing that the prefix *'in,'* is a Latin negative prefix, and *'un,'* is the English prefix. Utter nonsense.

The key word is alien, that comes from the word *lien*, the etymological root of which is the Anglo-French *lien*, meaning a loyen bond, restraint, from Latin *ligamen*, from *ligare* to bind.

Thus if *lien* means to bond, or bind, then its opposite connotation means to undo that bond; to alienate one aspect or element, from its other(s). Where a part cannot possibly be split, divorced, or separated, then the bond is <u>und</u>oable; it is <u>una</u>ble to be broken. Hence the word, <u>una</u>lienable, is utilised, to indicate that the bond is <u>una</u>ble to be severed, by any means whatsoever.

What then, is meant by the word *inalienable?* Most simply it means *not subject to being taken away from, or given away,* by the possessor. *Not subject to,* is worlds apart from *unable by any means.*

Is this distinction merely overlooked, or is it deliberately intended never to be understood? I submit, that this ambiguity is intentional, for not only will both words be regarded as the same, but also that few will ever learn what either word means in fact. That, as a deliberate ploy, permits people to believe that government is attendant upon their natural rights, when in fact, it only addresses the (so called) rights of (legal) citizens. We should wisely guard against being mislead by misconstrued vocabulary.

The self-evident fact that Man lives, is his right to live. Man's right to life is inherent in the meaning of life; not separately granted or bestowed.

> A right is a moral principle defining and sanctioning a man's freedom of action in a social context. —Ayn Rand [ix]

Man's right to life, is inseparable from his nature. It is the right to think, and act, the right to use and exercise one's faculties in support of life. It is the right to live free from molestation, and to protect that right. Every abrogation, or refusal of these facts, represents death in some form.

The (American) *Declaration of Independence,* was intended to place before Mankind the common sense of the subject, precisely the issue of *rights endowed by Man's Creator.* Jefferson phrased the document, explicitly stating that, *'the laws of nature and of nature's God,'* confirms that all Men are equally endowed by their Creator, with unalienable rights to *Life, Liberty and the pursuit of Happiness.* The phrase, *'pursuit of happiness,'* means the unalienable right of the individual to act in furtherance of his life, including the *actions of* acquiring, possessing, protecting, and disposing of property.

Jefferson, carefully chose the distributive plural (of) the word laws, to include *both the law of nature, and the law of God* who presides over nature. By using the two phrases, Jefferson declared that all men are equally endowed by their Creator with *unalienable rights.* Thus the *laws of nature*, and of *nature's God* found Man's unalienable rights. One's right to life is inherent, intrinsic, immutable, and unalienable.

> The natural rights of life and liberty are unalienable —
> Bouvier's Law Dictionary, 1856 Edition.

Unalienable Rights, embrace intrinsic moral law within Man's nature, specifically his right to use all of his faculties of life, to sustain and maintain it. That is the *Natural Law of Integrity.*

> It is impossible for any individual to sell, transfer or otherwise dispose of an "unalienable Right". It is impossible for you to take one of my "unalienable rights". It is likewise impossible for me to even voluntarily surrender, sell or transfer one of my "unalienable rights". Once I have something "unalienable," it's impossible for me to get rid of it. It would be easier to give up the color of my eyes or my heart than to give up that which is unalienable. —Alfred Adask [x]

Man is entrusted by Creator to honour his life, and those of all others. Jefferson stated that Man's *'rightful liberty, is drawn about each by the equal rights of all others.'* In consequence, Man is not lawfully permitted to initiate violence of any kind, or trespass another's right to life, but is morally free to defend himself, and arrest violent actions initiated by others.

To summarise, *Unalienable Rights* are immutable, impossible to erase, respectful of and within the equal rights of all others. They are Man's right to action; the immutable right of Man to live and sustain his life. No directive or proclamation of Man can erase this fact—but can violate it.

Inalienable Rights

The right to life is not self-ownership, as many will claim. One's life is no one's property; it is not even your property. One cannot (separately) own, what he or she already is. Consider this—

- Man has the unalienable right to his life, and to sustain it.
- To sustain it, he must be able to keep and own the proceeds of his effort—the fruits of his labour.
- If not, then his life-sustaining efforts are plundered, and his right to live is violated.

> The right to life is the source of all rights—and the right to property is their only implementation. Without property rights, no other rights are possible. Since man has to sustain his life by his effort, the man who has no right to the product of his effort has no means to sustain his life. The man who produces while others dispose of his product is a slave. Bear in mind that *the right to property is a right to action, like all the others: it is not the right to an object but to the action and the consequences of producing or earning that object. It is not a guarantee that a man will earn any property, but only a guarantee that he will own it if he earns it.* It is the right to gain, to keep, to use and to dispose of material values. — Ayn Rand[xi] [Emphasis mine]

The principle is clear, namely that the declared right to seek, and so to acquire property, is an unalienable right, encompassed and bound by the phrase, *'pursuit of happiness.'* However, one's unalienable *right to action*, is not, unalienable *right to its product*, or property, as described below.

Right to Property

John Locke (1632-1704), an English philosopher and political theorist, offered a very valid distinction concerning *property*. He said in effect, that land is a raw material to which the *'property of labour'* can be added, e.g., to improve a parcel of land. Thus, as permitted by Man's unalienable right to action, *'the land and his labour are joined such that the improved land, by the property of his effort, becomes his property.'*

The improved land is not Man's by unalienable right. *Right to property,* arises from adding labour to improve land, that prior Man's effort, (to use Locke's words,) is *'the state that Nature hath provided, and left it in.'*

Locke's idea conflicted with the Divine Right of Kings, wherein the king is the universal lord, and original proprietor of all the lands in his kingdom. That is what America's *founding fathers* sought to escape. Their tool was to expressly include *action*, including to improve land and one's life, by entering the phrase *'pursuit of happiness.'* In effect, the *Declaration of Independence* had grasped the significance of Locke's work, and in one phrase, encapsulated the natural laws concerning Mans life, his freedom to live it, and his right to enjoy the fruits of his labours.

Locke's context was wider than just land, however. In his *Classic Labour Theory of Private Property,* he asserted that *'the Labour of Mans Body, and the Work of his Hands, we may say, are properly his.'* Further, *'that whatsoever he removes out of the State that Nature hath provided, and left it in, he hath mixed his labour with, and*

144

joined to it something that is his own, and thereby makes it his property.'

Sir William Blackstone (1723-1780) agreed. He held that, *'bodily labour, bestowed upon any subject which before lay in common to all men, is universally allowed to give the fairest and most reasonable title to an exclusive property.'*

This applied principle means, that (manufactured) material products, unlike (non-manufactured) raw materials, inherently comprise a man or woman's (labour) efforts, that are inseparable from it. The effort, is the product of whosoever applied it, and remains so, even when ownership entitlement is transferred, i.e. when the product is sold, gifted, or bequeathed.

Rights defined

Unalienable rights as already defined, leaves *inalienable rights* floating in space absent definitive meaning. The works of Locke, Blackstone, and Jefferson, offer an inevitable conclusion, however. If Man has the *unalienable right to act in support of his life*, and his efforts do sustain his life, does he not have an incontestable *right to the products of his efforts*? Unequivocally yes!

Thus products can be sold, gifted, or bequeathed by choice, whereby (labour) efforts are automatically transferred because they are inherent *in* the product. The maker's incontestable right to the (product of) effort, transfers by his or her choice, in such cases. His or her right to the property, being property entitlement, transfers to the new owner.

One's *right to life*, versus one's *right to his or her life sustaining efforts*, is now unmistakable. The words *Unalienable*, and *Inalienable*, are objectively definable as never before.

- **An unalienable right** is Man's *right to action*; the unfettered right of Man to live and sustain his life, within the rights of all others.
- **An inalienable right** is Man's *right to the product of his action(s)*; the right of entitlement (or belonging) to that which his efforts have produced, including improvements (and cultivations) made to land.

Inalienable, means one's right to the property of effort contained *in* it — hence *in*alienable. When entitlement is sold or transferred, the word *inalienable* loses the prefix of *in,* precisely because the right of ownership has been transferred. Thus no matter how many times after that an item or product changes ownership, the new owner owns the product in full.

- Man's *right to act* in support of his life is *unalienable*.
- Man's *right to the product* of his efforts is *inalienable*.
- One may transfer ownership of the product of one's efforts to another, whereby the inalienable right to that product exchanges, for value.

Never, does anyone have a right to confiscate, usurp, plunder, defile, or steal any individual's *inalienable* right to their property. Property may be aliened, however.

The massive difference between *unalienable* and *inalienable* rights is very clear and immediate; its applicability fundamental, and far-reaching.

- *Unalienable rights* deny all Legal Entities and government instrumentalities from ruling Man. Man's right to life is unalienable; all trespass, violation and aggression of Man's right to life outlawed.
- *Inalienable rights* deny Legal Entities and government instrumentalities from confiscating Mans (lawful) property. The subject of one's property, an item, or product, can be

aliened, but one's (labour of love) right to it, never taken. Theft, and eminent domain, are outlawed.

Both unalienable and inalienable rights, belong to flesh and blood living beings. Both are divorced from today's legal jurisdiction. Right to action, and right to its product, cannot apply to inert fictional legal entities; because they cannot action anything. Thus *unalienable* and *inalienable* rights are categorically denied authoritative misappropriation, by anyone, any government, or any else, for any purpose.

Both of these rights, fall within the jurisdiction of natural law, respectful of independent living beings; all other jurisdictions or collectives prohibited.

Rights – Transfer of title

When *inalienable* property rights are lawfully transferred to a new owner, whether gifted, bequeathed or sold, the original (possessor's) *inalienable right* to it automatically converts to the new owner's *alienable right* to the property. The product retains its invested effort of course, but that effort belongs to the original owner, not its new owner. The right of ownership—*right of entitlement*—is transferred, but never is Man's inalienable right to own property relinquished, sacrificed or forsaken. (This has far-reaching implications, for contractual matters.)

Unalienable rights, and inalienable rights, must be forever preserved, and protected, including the right to *lawfully transfer ownership entitlement*. Products can be aliened, but never stolen, damaged or plundered, without consent.

Rights and natural justice

The above descriptions and reasons, I submit, are the most proper and lawful description of *inalienable rights* ever offered. Plagiarising, that has allowed inalienable rights, and unalienable rights to have the same meaning, is now overturned.

Although it may seem from these observations that inalienable rights, precede unalienable rights, both are co-dependent. You cannot have one without the other! The simple truth is, that a producer who does not own the result of his effort, whose production is usurped, or stolen, does not have the right to live. State denial of property rights, effectively turns men, and women, into property owned by the state.

Does this explain why *human rights* are be ruled by the United Nations, in contravention of its (Article 1) statement that, *'all human beings are born free and equal in dignity and rights'*?

> Whoever claims the "right" to "redistribute" the wealth produced by others is claiming the "right" to treat human beings as chattel. —Ayn Rand [10]

It is worth repeating, that without the right to sustain one's life, no right to life is possible. Without property rights, no other rights are possible.

Now the plunder of rights, and goods across centuries, is laid bare. Above descriptions, explain why those two very different phrases have been construed to mean the same thing. Consider for a moment. If, as a dictator (aka government), you could re-write the dictionary, and change *'unable by any means'* (unalienable) to imply *'not subject to'* (inalienable), and thereby write the rules of what is to be subject to what, you'd be laughing all the way to the bank, most surely?

Does that explain why states rule that *equitable title,* is separable from the *legal title*? Does that explain, why the Thomas Jefferson Memorial, in Washington DC, has the word INALIENABLE engraved in twelve inch high letters, despite that Jefferson used the word *Unalienable*?

Much mystery, ambiguity, falsity, belligerent assertions, and ideological stupidities will fall flat on their face, once it is understood that —

Unalienable right, is Man's right to action, so to sustain his life!

Inalienable right, is Man's right to the product of his life-sustaining actions! — and that free will cannot be usurped without one's consent.

Those definitions, are those used in this whole treatise. All others, including those in law dictionaries, are henceforth challenged to (differently) define Mans individual right to life, unalienable rights, and inalienable rights; entirely based on the nature of Man's life, and Creator's natural laws; all other founding premises, or standpoints irrelevant!

Protecting individual rights

Man's right to life, necessitates that he protect the right, to protect his rights. This understanding is imperative, crucial beyond measure. Virtually everyone who knows of the American *Declaration of Independence,* credits that document as the most definitive expose of Mans individual rights ever written. So it is. Its protections of Mans life, as an individual, and not as a social animal, are clear, unequivocal, and unambiguous.

Why then, has it not succeeded? Why is it not today's absolute standard? Having made such progress, what error, or omission, has allowed Mans right to his life to be usurped, overruled, rejected, reviled, repressed, stripped from existence and denied practical utility?

There seems only one answer. Nothing on the political horizon of 1776, could have suggested that it might be essential to protect the essence and nature of Mans (declared) protections, inherent in the document. Jefferson said so himself, did he not? *'We hold these truths to be self-evident.'* His conclusion, when viewed retrospectively, suggests that one's individual right to *life, liberty, and the pursuit of happiness*, once declared, are so self-evident and complete, that no need could ever exist to protect those rights.

History has exposed that shortcoming. It has shown that upholding one's right to life, and by corollary, the vital need to protect one's right to life, are two distinctly separate issues. Clearly, that fact was not self-evident in 1776, or such protection would have been included. Admittedly, Jefferson offered that *'whenever any form of government becomes destructive of these ends, it is the right of the people to alter or to abolish it.'* That clause is a vital truth, but sadly, it allows the horse to bolt before the gate closes.

In retrospect, we should have fully *protected our declared right*, to *claim that right*! We should have proclaimed that, *'the laws of nature and nature's God,'* (Jefferson's expression), not only pertain to our living being, but also to have insisted that our living being must protect the natural law. Why? Because while the *'laws of nature and nature's God'* are fixed, the content of Man's free will is not. Our right to act as individuals, includes the right to slap Creator's face; to reject natural law, and that, is Mans history.

If ever America's revered *Declaration of Independence* is to be to retrieved, an additional clause needs be added—specifically to protect Man's immutable, unalienable right to protect the right—to uphold his right to life. E.g.,

> To secure the certain, unalienable right to life, unless all men created equal, unequivocally ensure their right to life, and their unalienable right so to do against all cancellation, violation, or usurpation, they will have neither. —Kenneth Bartle

That clause best endorses Creator's *Natural Law of No Trespass*; also covered in the *Constitution of Man,* Chapter 22 — specifically Clause

1.9.1, that states — *'No exception shall ever exist, or an amendment made to Clauses 1 through 7 herein, inclusive.'*

Rightful society

Until the twentieth century, Locke's widely accepted position was well recognised; almost self-evident. Most particularly so when the state was unarmed, and the people were armed, as in eighteenth-century England, and America. History has shown that not only was Locke correct factually, but morally also. Locke, and other Christian advocates of natural law, accepted their accordance with the will of God, not because of divine revelation, or commandment, but because they rightfully concluded that the nature of Man, and the world, reflects the will of God. Similarly, I have described natural laws as Creator's *invitation to live,* as distinct from law as commandments.

It matters least, what name ascribes the source of our natural, orderly processes—Creator, God, Nature, Jehovah, or any other name. Most profoundly relevant, systems, patterns, and processes exist within our living nature. Moreover, that all directly bear on our body, mind and emotions, cooperatively, beneficially, spiritually, and without conflict, save by free choice. Such integrity of life-supporting purpose, is complete, in all respects. Altogether, these entirety describe a science of ethical morality within us, one that human sciences have seldom recognised before, much less described.

Very few have proffered such an idea. Ayn Rand, initially spoke of a *code of ethics* as an ideal. Later, she referred to it as a *science of ethics,* yet no one to my knowledge, has fully identified and expressed what core tenets that science should properly embrace.

We are indeed most fortunate. Whereas Creator has written a *Code of Ethics* within the natural laws of Mans very being, nothing ethical may be severed from his nature, else life suffers. What more, can Man's completeness teach?

151

My present expression of these natural laws may polish with time. Nonetheless, all conflict between *is,* and *ought,* that has baffled philosophers for centuries, is resolved. What Man spiritually *is,* determines what Man spiritually *ought* to do. If Man is to allow friendly societies, to replace authoritarian societies backed by violence, what better than Creator's *Science of Ethics,* indelibly written in the nature and life of Man?

It's a very simple choice. Will you accept Creator's invitation to live, in freedom and full mastery of your life, respectful of the lives of all others? Or will you kowtow to authority, including to be forcibly punished, even by death, so that the state will survive at the expense of all but itself?

17

INITIATED AND RETALIATORY FORCE

Non-Agression

Life itself, requires that no one may trespass another's individual right to his, or her life. Libertarians most often refer to this idea, as the Non-aggression Principle (NAP), this being an ethical stance asserting that (initiated) aggression is inherently illegitimate, or wrongful.

Aggression, for this purpose, is defined as starting, or threatening the use of any and all forcible interference with an individual's life, or an individual's property. For this, *the non-aggression principle,* admits that violent *self defence* is legitimately lawful.

The NAP is fundamentally sound in principle. Force, initiated by one against another, is wrongfully anti-life, so its arrest is rightfully pro-life. Notice the switch in focus, however. The primary issue is *not* the arresting of force, aggression, or violence, but the *living of life*! The most essential matter, is the *unalienable right* of every single man, and woman, *to live.* Until that condition holds supremacy, all discussion concerning the cessation of violence, puts the cart before the horse.

Life should found Man's ethical thinking and moral actions. One's (individual) unalienable right to life takes precedence. All discourse concerning aggression, or its arrest, is subsequent.

Moral justness served to others, is Creator's guarantee that Mans freedom to live is always within his grasp and fulfilment.

Morality – Blanket coverage

Morality has long been considered a *social ethic*. Monarchs, tyrants, state, church, and society, have long specified moral standards for all to conform to, and why not? Taught that Man is a social animal to be ruled, morality is useful tool to that social end.

Now invert that notion in your mind. Forget its communal derivation, morality as a collective ideal. Divorce singular men and women from the *collective,* and accord their true nature as an independent living being. Then, morality is instantly snatched from the social arena, and restored to independence where it rightfully belongs. Every man, woman, and child, is the author of their personal morality, or immorality, and accountable for it. That is because actions are of their sovereign choice. Morality or immorality, spring forth from every individual man and woman, not from blanket edicts invented by self-proclaimed moralists, governments, or as interpreted by Man from God's laws.

Why must morality blanket mankind, as it does today? Arguably because, unless morality is made uniform, it can have no unified effect. Purportedly, Man would run amok were morality left to each individual; the same premise that claims Man must be ruled by a government. Thus imposed laws, and moral dictates, are accepted without question, almost universally believed to provide security, comforts, and protections. The fact that rules and commandments plunder Man's life, seems irrelevant or inconsequential, because no alternative seemingly exists.

So, many will scream indignantly, *'how can uniform moral uprightness be achieved if each chooses their own?'* The answer is simple. There is no such thing as a moral collective, or society, but an aggregate of moral individuals is possible.

> Morality, is nothing but your conscious will to live according to your nature, never depriving others the same opportunity.
> —Kenneth Bartle

That's what the NAP desires, but it's focus is misdirected. Violence, and aggression, are not *social disorders*. They are *personal disorders*. Aggression, is one's actioned interference, trespass, or violation of another's individual's right to life—or life-sustaining property. Of course violence can be committed by groups, or collections of individuals, governments included. Notwithstanding, all government decisions spring from one individual human being—joint congressional, or parliamentary decisions notwithstanding—executive orders most emphatically. One person, signs the statute into law. No living being, who enacts an (invented) puppet role, or position granted by positive law, or *society by company,* is excused, or exonerated. (Witness decisions given at the Nuremberg Trials.) No government is exempt.

Mans life and nature, and particularly its natural laws, prove the foundations of ethics, morality, and justice. Given (free will) right by Creator to accept, or reject legislative orders, one's personally committed actions manifestly confess one's agreed (moral) responsibility for them. Living beings push buttons, write letters, eat food, or poisons, and experience outcomes—fictional entities cannot—they're lifeless.

Arrest of aggression, is indeed of vital concern, but until Man's individual, unalienable *right to life* holds precedence, the principal of *non-aggression* lacks definitive backbone reference. Switch focus to *one's right to life,* and protection of life necessarily and automatically follows.

155

Initiation of physical force

Life's protection, invites questions. What constitutes the kind of interference that trespasses or violate an individual's right to life? Ayn Rand cut through centuries of confusion concerning rights, by stating…

> To violate man's rights means to compel him to act against his own judgment, or to expropriate his values. Basically, there is only one way to do it: by the use of physical force.

And, conversely—

> Freedom, in a political context, has only one meaning: the absence of physical coercion.—Ayn Rand [xii]

Freedom means the protection of one's life and property, from interference, or trespass by others, specifically through physical force or coercion. Physical force is well understood; rape, bodily harm, detention, torture, and murder offer typical examples. Physical coercion, includes such as theft, legally or otherwise, blackmail, fraud, debilitating threats of violence, including all that arrests one's choice to do other than is forcibly commanded.

The basic principle of morality, and of justice, is that no man may initiate the use of physical force against others.

> Whatever may be open to disagreement, there is one act of evil that may not, the act that no man may commit against others and no man may sanction or forgive. So long as men desire to live together, no man may initiate—do you hear me? no man may start—the use of physical force against others.

> Men have the right to use physical force only in retaliation and only against those who initiate its use. The ethical principle involved is simple and clear-cut: it is the difference between murder and self-defense. A holdup man seeks to gain a value, wealth, by killing his victim; the victim does not

grow richer by killing a holdup man. The principle is: no man may obtain any values from others by resorting to physical force. —Ayn Rand [xiii]

Creator's *Natural Law of NoTrespass* forbids physical force initiated against others—thus *non aggression as a principle* is fully covered, without needing Man's written rules.

> A right cannot be violated except by physical force. Whenever a man is made to act without his own free, personal, individual, voluntary consent—his right has been violated.
>
> We can draw a clear cut division between the rights of one man and those of another. It is an objective division—not subject to differences of opinion, nor to majority decision, nor to the arbitrary decree of society. No man has the right to initiate the use of physical force against another man. — Ayn Rand [12]

In practice, no Man, group, society or government has the right to assume the role of a criminal, to initiate the use of physical compulsion against any man, woman, or child. When advocates of the non-aggression principle (NAP) hail Mans *right to life* as primary, seek first to institute and protect it, their cause will advance immeasurably.

Retaliatory Force

Man's willingness to agree that he is a *social animal*, is devastating. It has crippled his mind to blindly accept centuries of physical, mental, and emotional harm, perpetrated by *authority* and backed by deadly force.

How did this happen? By agreeing the social animal lie, and never challenging social authority that herds us all. We should have known better! We should have busted the herd mentality millennia ago, yet today its truth remains unknown to all but very few.

> Do not open your mouth to tell me that your mind has
> convinced you of your right to force my mind. Force and mind
> are opposites; morality ends where a gun begins. When you
> declare that men are irrational animals and propose to treat
> them as such, you define thereby your own character and
> can no longer claim the sanction of reason—as no advocate
> of contradictions can claim it. —Ayn Rand [24]

Force is one of two kinds therefore.

1. Initiated force that violates one's life is unlawful, unjust and immoral.
2. Defensive arrest of unlawful and destructive force so as uphold life. Such (arresting) force is lawful, just, and moral.

Isn't this the non-aggression principle? No. Why not? Because life is the moral issue, whereby the extent, and degree of retaliatory force, are determined by the aggressor, not by a defendant, or judge.

That is Creator's *Natural Law of No Trespass*. The difference between morality as a social convention, and its proper place within each (individual) living being, becomes vibrantly clear. Morality exists within every cell, tissue, organ, system, and our conscious and subconscious minds. It has existed since Mans inception, and life demands that we protect it.

> If physical force is to be barred from social relationships,
> men need an institution charged with the task of protecting
> their rights under an objective code of rules. —Ayn Rand [24]

That was to have been the role of government. Not one government In all history has done so. No government has fully upheld the concept of Individual Rights. America came closest.

Change is needed

Nothing will change, until Man divorces himself from the insanity of an animalistic society, ruled by tyrants with a pen in one hand and a gun in the other! Those who declare that Men are irrational animals, and forcibly treat them as such, are outlaws by their own (action based) confession. They are the aggressors—the terrorists. They have forsaken morality. Their success, helped by your ignorance of their crimes, derives from widespread, unchallenged acceptance of *Man as a social*. These criminals are protected at your expense, and know it. Most people do not. Fortunately, they are in the minority.

Time has come, to end this era of ignorance and all that it permits. It is time to declare that your life is sacrosanct, and inviolable, and so is your right to protect it. Please see the *Commission of Justice* at www.naturalelaw.com. It replaces government, and is strictly prohibited from making rules and enforcing them. The Commission's sole function is to protect Mans unalienable right to life, to arrest the initiated use of physical force against others, and dispense justice.

Revolutionary independence

A whole new life-supporting perspective emerges. Singularity of life-purpose annihilates duality. It vanishes. Life is the only goal and purpose. Wrong and evil do not disappear; they merely present as uncivil or criminal deviations, from the cause and purpose of life. They are not the equal of life. They are not equitable competitors. They are entirely gutless, nuisance like diseases, manifesting as abusive aberrations. Nonetheless, they require correction, and remediation.

So presents a new understanding contrary to almost all taught. It begs a complete re-appraisal of psychology, psychiatry, philosophy, religion, politics, trade, society, competition and cooperation. It challenges commonly held beliefs, religions, politics and subjectivism. It throws authoritative government on the scrap heap. It even challenges the libertarian persuasion, to reappraise their goals. It also begs that we redefine justice, based on the Natural Law of Allowance, and *Just Consequence*. Almost every precept ever taught is called into question!

How can this be? The simple answer, is that Mans life is Creator's desire and endowment. However, because Man inverted it, invented and wrote rules to controvert it, so it is now up to you and me, to steer it back on course.

It's not the independence of one state from another, such as the 1776 *Declaration of Independence*. It is each man, and each woman's independence, from any state that violates their right to life.

Its core premise is that you are a unique individual, that your life is your life. Every statement declaring otherwise, reveals that authors deviation from the purpose of their life, often for nefarious purposes. Criminals require remediation. Those who uphold their life respectful of others do not.They understand the *Natural Laws of Respect and Integrity, the Law of No Trespass, and the Law of Just Consequence,* in full. They choose to live according to natural law ethics, because such are Creator's keys to success.

All men and women have free choice, to (ethically) know in advance of any action, exactly what potential consequence will result. According to one's choices, morality or immorality is publicly manifested by one's actions. Once the deed is done, the author is accountable for it.

A symbiotic society may thus emerge. Symbiosis, broadly defines as the interaction between two different organisms living in close physical association, typically to the advantage of both. Cooperation, and collaboration emerge as primary considerations, but let's proceed with caution.

18

FROM ETHICS TO MORALITY

Ethics

Ethics, as a discipline, investigates, recommends, systematises and defends concepts of right and wrong conduct. Prior described in a thousand religious and political ways, here in context, *right* upholds and sustains one's life. All else is anti-life, meaning *wrong*.

The term ethics derives from the Ancient Greek word *ethikos,* that stems from the word ethos (habit, custom).

Ethical study, embraces praxeology, which is concerned with the nature of value, and valuation, and of the kinds of things that are valuable. Thus ethics are a formulation of a *code of value* and evaluation, that presupposes the question—of value to whom and for what? Man, for the sake of living his life, is the correct answer.

Are you joining the dots? Remember how the infant in my example programmed *value* into its subconscious mind, and what it achieved, without math, vocabulary, or cognitive ability. Rejoice that you accomplished the same success. Remember how the *3x1 minute program* focusses on impressing *value* on the subconscious mind. Recall how you *imaged your success,* and how your subconscious mind affirmatively acknowledged your desires, via mentoring ability.

Remember above all, that every success resulted from your choice to pursue it—most failures from not planning. Never forget how choice is yours, and that when you consciously charge subconscious mind with your values, you request its inestimable power. (Oops if you do not.)

Remember all those lessons and, no doubt will exist in your mind that a *science of ethics* is entirely objective and personal. All else is divisive and irrelevant.

Watch out. Virulent accusations of karma, ego, selfishness, and many more debilitating blinders, will seek to deter you from pursuing the cause of self, all pleading your agreement in a vague and non-conclusive manner.

Fortunately, your free will holds the ace card. Hopefully, by now, you've proven that personal success is within your realm and ability. You've already shown yourself, that life-values are crucial to your physical, mental, emotional, and spiritual joy. Henceforth, every proposition or goal may add to your mental, and spiritual growth, by the same means.

That explains *ethics* and the vital need for ethical considerations.

Ethics comprise three major areas of study, today, vis—

- **Meta-ethics**—which deals with the theoretical meaning and reference of moral propositions, including how truth values, if any, can be determined.
- **Normative ethics**—which deals with the means of determining a moral course of action.
- **Applied Ethics**—which concerns ethical practices, written for lawyers, doctors, and like professions. (I've avoided this topic, because real morality supplants it in context.)

Accordingly, Meta-ethics is my first concern and focus based on the nature and life of Man. Normative ethics follow—this being one's personal undertaking, correctly based on Meta-ethic principles. Since natural laws empower each being to function as Creator intentioned, then by proper extrapolation, they should also apply to ethics, and morality, regarding his social and business dealings.

Ethics is deserted

The Dark and Middle Ages, are a testimonial monument to the *mystical theory of ethics*, later replaced by a *social theory of ethics*. This, widely accepted as a social theory for the collective. Call it society, human rights, an ideal for Mans benefit, or goodwill. Preach that unity, altruism, or Mans ethical duty is to be the selfless, voiceless, slave of any need, claim, or demand asserted by others.

Subjectivism thrives on this mystical premise. Its compass of reality is fluid, plastic, and indeterminate. Broad consensus is the final arbiter, whereby Man needs no definitive policies, objective values, personal ethics, and no individual morality. Church, or state, will determine all, or we'll hold a referendum and let the collective have its say. So it is believed that *consensus* must control the *social animal*. Existential monument to this theory of intellectual vacuum, and vagrancy, is witnessed by the present state of today's culture, political and otherwise. Responsibility, for the collective base of ethics, belongs entirely to the philosophers of altruism. They, and their disciples, sought to avert natural justice. They seduced, mind-managed, cajoled, threatened, forced, and even blackmailed Man to obey their edicts of universal morality. Man agreed; no other choice seemingly presented.

Natural justice, has justly replied in exact measure of this damnable, and criminal violation of Mans right to life. Meta-ethics and normative ethics were smashed. Applied ethics remained, being ethical professional practices written for lawyers, doctors, and medical businesses, even for social policies and institutions. Are they for you and me? No. All focus on upholding the stature of their respective (commercial) enterprises. Applied ethics, are little more than fanciful *terms and conditions* pleading universal moral endorsement. That is not to criticise their value, but to emphasise that when personal ethics, and responsibility are sacrificed to authority, or consensus, few can tell the difference.

An *Objective Code of Ethics*, first credited to Ayn Rand, and although spoken of by several authors, has not been fully expressed, or described. Here, I will attempt to fill that vacancy in principled terms.

When philosophers declare that reason has failed, that ethics is beyond the power of reason, and that no rational ethics can ever be defined, what then remains? Faith, instinct, propaganda, revelation, feelings, beliefs, urges, and whims fill the void. Does it matter, that folk invent fancy titles such as arbitrary postulate, subjective evaluation, emotional commitment, unity consciousness or alchemical transformation? Not one bit. When ethics is *subjective*, reason, and mind, surrender to an empty wilderness of non-defined phrases, stolen concepts, meaningless, and incomprehensible verbiage. Such do little but regurgitate bereft age-old philosophies, in modern day vernacular, to be swallowed by the masses. Thus deprived, Man is cast aside, left to perish in a nonsensical vacuum, taught and believed to be *enlightening*.

Happy to fill this void, state and church agree, that morality is a necessary component of civil authority, for which they, are the prescribers of right and wrong, As self-proclaimed authors, they hold themselves to be the *authority of morality*; that includes *the moral right to rule,* and *the immoral wrong to refuse rule.*

No more deadly formula exists. It is absolutely lethal! Man-made laws, authoritatively prescribe morality, and back it with (legal) force, *that utterly forbids it being moral.* Man falls for this criminal insanity—and pays for it most dearly—because morality, as taught, approves of it! Thus Man is to agree the *moral right to rule, and immoral wrong to refuse rule,* without question.

Men and women, as unique singular beings of Creation, are thereby swept aside as of no consequence, and no importance. Governments profit, from contrived legal criminality that grants their right to rule. So it is, that most people are totally oblivious of the fact, that *we each have an unalienable moral right, to refuse commandment from anyone.*

Every edict, instruction, coercion, statute law, or commandment from governments are intended to conceal Man's moral necessity to think individually, do, and act for his benefit and life—instead to uphold the state. Today's trauma's, the slavery of billions, the pain, suffering, and death of thousands, daily or weekly, *is not the failure of morality; it is the inescapable consequence of denying morality.*

Denial of the *individual rights of Man* infringes the reality of his existence, that is *fully immoral.* No one is exempt from morality, most especially governments.

Immoral authority

Many will not be satisfied by that explanation. Consensus morality, is morally imperative, most folk will argue; as in *'how could one man, or one woman, ever prescribe morality, given others will most likely hold different opinions?'* Is that a good question? No, sorry, it's a tragic misunderstanding.

Universal morality, ordinarily taught from childhood by parents and grandparents, is later reinforced by religious persuasion, and through positive law, aka the legal system. Communal morality, is pressed into Mans mindset as the unchallengeable truth. Because it is considered to be moral, its professed truth is held unquestionable.

When those who dissent from this position, are contemptuously charged with advocating immorality, who will have the courage to speak their *moral mind,* with certitude? Precious few! Lets look at this from a different perspective. *If I act in support of my life, or I violate yours, which of my actions is moral, and who decided it; me, or some self-appointed moralist?'*

'But, but, but,' it might be protested, *'moralists are trained to determine what is moral, and what is not, so who are you to know better?'*

That retort illustrates how *the mindset of authority* takes root. Moralists, should have long understand morality to its fullest degree. That is their vocation after all. Inclusive in their education, and in their mind, should be that by natural law, *commandment of another's mind is immoral.* That some actions uphold life, and some do not, does not by natural law, allow for one's choice to be ruled by force. Any morality that asserts authority to command, is immoral!

Rebellion

Rebellion of authority by teenagers, often demonstrates this aspect very transparently. Precisely because parents have long accepted authority as the term-setter of morality, they often fail to grasp that their teenage son, or daughter, has no desire to reject their moral advice wilfully, but instead the idea that *authority rules morality.* Arguments will often arise, because neither party is able to express that morality comes from within. Parents have accepted the contrary, that society determines what is moral. Meanwhile, the teenager feels a desperate longing to experience life, learn, and thus determine what morally concurs. He, or she, struggles valiantly to discover moral guidance from within, as they should, but is taught instead, that right and wrong are prescribed by others. Thus the teenager's every attempt to express their free will thoughts and ideas, is crushed, in the name of conforming to blanket morality, and authority.

Endeavours to grasp their beautiful nature, are smashed. Parents cannot understand the teen's quest for free expression. Indoctrinated submission to authority, which they have accepted, precludes it. All too often, the teen is forced to bow to state power, which sacrifice of their moral choices are, the approval that government wants—about which parents know little or nothing.

Truth seeking minds smash into a brick wall. They break. They freak out, their tender growth into a beautiful adult being, regularly arrested. Too often they cannot mentally handle, what their inquiries show to be belligerent, bloody-minded insanity. Escape at all cost becomes imperative; the only course available. Professional health workers, who fervently seek to understand drug use, should question how much arises from mind-bending dictatorship, hailed as moral.

Science of ethics, and morality

'*How on earth, will errant moral behaviour be arrested, if each is his or her moral governor,*' folk will scream indignantly. The answer lies in the *Natural Law of Just Consequence*. It confirms that the instigator of an immoral action, publicly confesses guilt through his or her action(s). One's actions publicly admit moral, or immoral standing. Intentions come first of course, but actions cause harm, not thoughts.

Two sciences suggest, vis—

- **A science or code of ethics**, devoted to *how men, and women, should think* of life-values and life itself, respectively for self and of others.
- **A science or code of morality,** describing *how men, and women, should act*, based on the science or code of ethics, respective of self and the lives of all others.

Ethics concerns thinking, reasons, and values. Ethical choices precede actions, that express morality or immorality, as rights and wrongs of social behaviour. Ethics concerns thought, and intention, while morality is subsequent action.

By ascribing *ethics to the thought* process, and *morality to actions* three things result.

- Ethics and morality are separated, one from the other.
- Morality concerns actioned results, not prior (ethical) intentions.
- Both are removed from the collective social arena, and placed squarely in the (individual) personal domain.

Now, the above descriptions assume much greater relevance.

Meta-ethics

Without life, ethics is an empty or invalid concept, because *value* is absent. Given that Man's reasoning faculty, must determine what may be of value to his life, versus what is not, then ethics is wholly determined by each individual. So the question—of value to whom, and for what—is fully answered. Man's life is the standard of value, for all ethical deliberation, in order to live it. It cannot be expressed any simpler.

This principle is vital and yet so simple, specifically—*Life demands that one always act to support and sustain it, never sacrificing its supreme value to something lesser.* Every ethical consideration of Man, every desire, goal, and purpose, are embraced by that statement. Free will is key. Meta-ethics correctly appraises values, and chooses accordingly. None are automatic. One can decide to be ethical, or unethical. One can evaluate, choose, reconsider, and choose anew. No one is affected, no harm occasioned but to oneself, Only one's actions can harm others.

Normative ethics

Beyond exploring possibilities, normative ethics is more purposefully concerned with one's chosen commitment to effect a result. It remains as one's freely chosen ethical choice, however, up and until it is enacted.

Ethical, or unethical persuasions are acted upon, or rejected, whereby no action occurs. Thus normative ethical considerations prompt action, that manifest one's morality. Because we each are the normative author of our actions, each is the absolute originator of their morality. Each is fully accountable. No other jurisdiction applies.

The relationship between *self-contained ethics,* and *publicly expressed morality,* is now very clear.

Meta-ethics, deals with the meaning and reference of ethical propositions, and their truth values. Normative ethics, determine a moral course of action. Both ethics, and morals, are individual in origin; arising from within each man and woman. They are not written for the collective, and blanket applied to Mankind, but usefully serve as advisory sciences, most assuredly.

- **Ethically:** Life demands the *wilful choice to support* and sustain it, never sacrificing its supreme value to anything lesser.
- **Morally:** Life impels that one *never act to deprive* another of his or her life or the means to support and sustain it.

Morality vs Law

Only now, can ethics be reunited with morality. Morality is not, and cannot be a social edict yet today's much supported *moral theory of jurisprudence* runs contrary. It maintains that (blanket applied) law defines morality, and ethics, that which is consensually held as rightful. This is to say, that because reason chooses between good and evil, so natural law finds its power in the finding of certain universal standards of morality and ethics.

Which comes first? Does morality determine what natural law is? Or do ethics, and morality, derive from discovered natural laws? Consider, that if natural law proceeds from some acclaimed morality, then self-proclaimed moralists presume the right to determine what natural law is. Their version of morality then rules, that universally denies or overrules what is independently natural. Haven't we got morality back to front, the cart before the horse?

Today's *moral theory of jurisprudence* appears immoral in both substance and principle. The sequence, whereby orderly process invokes *ethical thinking*, which later expresses as a moral action, is irreversible. Simply stated, every ethic needed in support of personal life, lies within every man and woman, on tap for his societal dealings with others.

It is as though Creator has said *'I have perfected societal governing within your very self, precisely so that you may translate those "Natural Laws" into your societies.'*

What better could Man ask? Natural laws are within the nature and science of Man, while free will determination of value, and purpose, is spiritual. Each interfaces the other. This bond, endorses that Man is *a spiritual being living a spiritual life*, albeit in a physical body and environment.

The Golden Rule

We're all familiar with the adage, the so-called golden rule, *do unto others as you would have them do unto you.* Everyone preaches it, yet natural law does not support it. Its creed, is collectivism, not individuality and free will independence. Purportedly an example to others, it imparts the idea that others actions must found on your morality, or as you approve. Vice versa, you must act according to their moral choices. (So, burgle others as you would have them burgle you.)

No quicker shortcut to a subjective morality exists—dare I suggest that is its purpose. When morality is subjective, up for grabs to all comers, no life supporting guidance, or morality exists.

The so-called golden rule may be re-written, paraphrased thus— *Do morally unto yourself as you would others do justly unto themselves.* Then your actions will tell of your noble intentions, your moral stature, and speak of your love of life. You lead by example, and while that may infer that others should follow, their moral choice is entirely their own, including consequence.

This principle already exists within you—beautifully shown by mentoring reports (emotions) being justly delivered for your conscious learning—if you so choose. Creator has modelled the principle of *natural justice*, smack in the core of our conscience, and emotional reporting systems, exactly where it belongs!

Once grasped, that ethics are consideration of one's desires in life-value terms, and that morality or immorality is outwardly broadcast to all others, no difficulty should experience in freely choosing a just path, with beneficial consequences.

(Please pay close attention to the words *justness* versus *justice* hereafter—both are defined and given their proper place.)

19

JUSTNESS AND JUSTICE

Justness prefaces justice

Whereas justness, or unjustness, is served by one's actions, *justice serves remedy,* when needed. The difference between *justness* and *justice* is evident. Actions may or may not serve *justness* upon others. *Justness,* is morality in effect. *Unjustness* is immorality. *Justice* is different. It exists to correct immoral, unjust actions; the practice of remediating unjustness.

Questions. Should *justice* dictate morality? Do (today's) law courts administer justice? Do their decisions uphold morality, lawfulness, and respect for life, or are we grossly misled? Common sense begs several more questions.

Should (restorative) *justice* be given its proper place as correction, or remedy? If so, why shouldn't *moral justness,* be preemptively taught in the classrooms of 7-year-olds? Could *justness,* instilled in the minds and hearts of everyone, from an early age, put the practice of *justice* almost entirely out of business?

Observe the difference. Present practice begs we act morally from duty, or obligation, to achieve social ends, as administered by *society by company.* The alternative is to act pre-emptively, not because it's the dutiable human, or social thing to do, but because ethics facilitate personal spiritual growth, and advancement in our material world, that morally spills into our societies.

Expressed differently again, the physical *is* of Man should not determine what he *ought* morally to do, rather that his *spiritual is* should determine what he *ought morally, and spiritually to enact.*

Grasp that *spiritually founded natural laws, advance material life,* and all falls into place. Right reasoning, rational thinking, evaluation, integrity, purpose, and value selection based on life, emerge as a spiritually based Science of Ethics, its core tenets already written by Creator, most graciously, within all of us.

Do you see? Ethical justness, and personal morality, have every (free will) opportunity to excel. Every man and woman, has free choice to embrace the will to live, and employ its necessities. Justness serves oneself, and all others. It cannot fail.

Unethical thoughts give rise to wrong, immoral actions. Immorality, and unjustness, invoke remediation. If a man, or woman transgresses, because he or she has purposefully forsaken ethics and morality, nothing but restoration of moral order (and possible remediation) remains. That is the role of *natural justice.*

A code of ethics

Here summarised is an objective science and spiritually based Code of Ethics. (It may be written differently, of course, provided its core tenets remain.)

- **Life:** Nothing is more pertinent to every man, woman, or child on earth, than life. Life is the base reference for all that concerns it, including the natural laws of identity, causality, independence, respect, equality, integrity, individual rights, free will and commitment.

- **Virtues:** Virtues are attitudes, values, or developed character traits, that enable us to act in life-supporting ways that foster, and master our potential. These uphold our spiritual essence, embraced by all the above mentioned natural laws.
- **Respect:** Respect is the voluntary endorsement of the vital need to support one's life by lawful exercise of one's faculties. Respect applies to others reciprocally, since their wellbeing is reflective of one's own. Respect is entirely premised on Individual Rights, for without the individual right to one's life, one cannot respect the individual rights of all others. Respect embraces all the above mentioned natural laws.
- **Justness:** Justness is the sum of just actions, a testament of one's morality. Justness is reliant on the *Natural Law of Just Consequence*, that culminates as *Natural Justice,* uniting every natural law.

Life, Justness, Respect, and Virtues are internalised principles that found judgments of right and wrong—the objective, scientific, (Meta-ethic) discovery and defining of a moral code embracing principles of life supporting conduct. Those qualities embrace all the natural laws of and within oneself, accepting of all consequence, beneficial or otherwise. All pertain to each, as individuals, independent one from another, respective of one's desires, goals, ambitions, productivity, and life-sustenance.

Altogether they form a *Science of Ethics*, a foundation for life-sustaining morality.

A code of morality

A perfect sequential order becomes apparent; ethics first, and morality second. Here is a summation of a spiritually objective Code of Morality. (It may be written differently provided its core tenets remain.)

- **Morality:** Morality is the outward manifestation, of ethically based principles underpinning one's life-sustaining actions.

By contrast, immorality manifests lack, or refusal of ethical considerations, lack of moral discipline, or lack of justness. Thus one's moral stature embraces the totality of respect for self, and all others; immoral stature its refusal.

- **Protection**: The unalienable right to one's life, and inalienable right one's property, necessitates protection of individual rights; else individual rights amount to nought. Protection of the these rights arbitrates just restoration, when needed. Man's need for protection embraces the *Natural Laws of equality, morality, no trespass, and just consequence*.

- **Convivial Society**: Convivial society results from moral actions in aggregate. Independence, one from another, joins with respect for each other. Co-operation amongst equals, or one's likes, results in a mutual advantage. Cooperative enterprise embraces the *Natural Laws of integrity, morality, no trespass, efficacy, just consequence, and protection*. Convivial Society is thus founded on the spiritually objective Code of Ethics, and Morality by extension.

- **Living Justice**: Those who prize ethics, and morality, as spiritual progenitors of life, relish just consequence, and natural justice, as the steering virtues of life; founders of respect and unceasing justness when dealing with others. Fully understanding, that *Natural Justice* steers recalcitrants back to upholding moral actions, and the progress of convivial society, so they do all to uphold it. No law of Man can surpass this win-win accomplishment, for which all are enabled to know the consequences of their actions in advance.

The societal circle is now complete, just as Man is whole in himself. To arrive at anything less, would confess errors in one's thinking, or lack. A just, and convivial society, is not possible unless premised on individual rights, and natural law, including natural ethics and morality, inherent in Mans being. That is the reason and purpose of this thesis, the naturalelaw.com website, the *Constitution of Man*, and *Commission of Justice*.

Crime is the natural offspring of an unjust society

Arrest the initiation of force and violence, and convivial societal order opens to the light of day. Each man and woman, is not just another human, merely. Each one is a unique and precious being, governed by the natural laws of their nature. Their right to live, is exclusively independent, and immutable. Their life is theirs. Their singularity, their beautiful uniqueness, and the natural order of their life, ordains boundaries separating one human being from another; his or her rights, words, deeds, works, and property, from another's, and from other things.

Nothing could be simpler, or more in tune with nature herself.

20

LIVING JUSTICE

If *justness,* describes just actions, and *justice* is the remediation of unjust actions, then what exactly determines what is just, or unjust? Todays political ideology is not principally concerned with true justice for Man, rather it is the work of pragmatic, political ideologues, who have capitalised counterfeit philosophies suiting their own ends. Justice upholds the state today, not Man.

Here is the root of this plague.

- **Plato:** (c.429–c.347 bc), Greek philosopher. He, and a long string of political disciples, even to this day, have argued that *although likeness, equality, was indeed a fact, people ought to be taught otherwise.* So they would accept the different benefits, and burdens, arising from various positions in a politically organised society. Mans equality is thereby squashed. Political positions preside.
- **Aristotle:** (384–322 bc), a Greek philosopher and scientist, supported this view by arguing, that *likeness is but a superficial illusion.*
- **Rousseau:** (1712–78), French philosopher and writer, born in Switzerland. He believed that civilisation warps the fundamental goodness of human nature, and that while human freedom is a fact of nature, people should be taught to

consider that it is dangerous; whereby *they ought to sacrifice their individual nature to the artificial condition of citizenship.* According to Rousseau, *natural persons should become artificial persons, i.e. citizens —wittingly or unwittingly— willingly or by legal compulsion.* Many socialists agree.

- **Auguste Comte:** (1798–1857), the philosopher who coined the term altruism, stated that *'to live for others is for all of us a constant duty, the definitive formula of human morality.'* Comte further argued, that we *'cannot tolerate the notion of rights, for such notion rests on individualism.'* Thus arose his altruistic premise, that rights are as absurd as they are immoral and, *'individuals have a moral obligation to serve others and place their interests above one's own.'* Comte's fundamental assertion, was that people had to be altruistic to be moral, and fully selfless to be altruistic.

- **Karl Marx:** (1818–83), a German political philosopher and economist, endorsed a universal socialism, asserting that only the human species can be free; no independent being can be. *Individual freedom is an illusion*, he claimed. Marx called those who identify themselves with mankind as a whole, to be universal individuals. These species-beings, he argued, who know themselves to be identical with the human race, are true communists, representing the superior evolution of Mankind. Moreover, *they should not be dissuaded by illusions of morality and justice, among those still mired in the false consciousness of their particular individuality.*

- **John Dewey:** (1859–1952), American philosopher, father of pragmatism and modern liberalism. He explained the collectivist notion as—

- 'Society in its unified and structural character is the fact of the case; the non-social individual is an abstraction arrived at by imagining what man would be if all his human qualities were taken away. *Society, as a real whole, is the normal order, and the mass as an aggregate of isolated units is the fiction.'* [Emphasis mine.]

That last sentence, is opposite of all this book has described thus far. Join the dots. Today's politicians, and power-seekers, are empowered by this centuries-long chain of ideological collectivism, as above. They have *little need to debunk individualism, given above rhetoric, because no such thing is considered by professed experts to exist, or that should exist.* Many new age devotees are likewise beguiled, often espousing oneness, or collective consciousness.

Unsurprisingly, *lawmakers* will happily claim prestigious grasp of the (above referenced) ideologies among fellow *intellectuals,* so to justify regulations in flagrant violation of the principles of natural justice. Thereby, *injustice* incestuously feeds itself, while masses are fed more government handouts, bolstering an authoritarian nanny state upholding injustice, and immorality.

Here lies solid truth, that seems to have eluded man for millennia…

While ever it is *ruled wrong* to rape, pillage and plunder, *so rule,*that rapes, pillages and plunders, *is upheld to be right.*

Inverted morality, and corrupt justice no better explained, we stupidly fall for both. As taught and accepted, we praise our *rulers* for their correction of injustice, never for one-second understanding that rule is unjust. We tacitly swallow all they say, and vote at the polling booth to uphold injustice. They know of this, and tremble in terrible fear of the day that you know it; for their empire will collapse.

Top-down control, is the seat of (today's) collectivised injustice. The state rules, while (so-called) *justice* is charged with upholding it. Natural justice is apparent meanwhile, only by its absence.

Wisdom from that era

We should not write off periods of olden day history as tragic, altogether. Much of value offered.

Josiah Warren, (1798-1874), chose to pursue individualism. Indeed Benjamin Tucker who spoke of Warren as his *friend and master,* credits Warren with being *the first man to expound and give form to what is now known as Anarchism.* John Stuart Mill offered, that Warren recognised no authority for society, over the individual, save to ensure equal freedom for them all. Sovereignty of the individual, later became an important focus of Mill and Spencer.

So also, the work of Herbert Spencer, (1820-1903), an English sociologist, should not be forgotten. As a radical individualist, moral and political philosopher, he argued *absolute ethics* in his political and moral theory, specifically that violence and coercion is morally wrong, For some reason however, he also gave the state autonomy.

Neither should we omit the work of Lysander Spooner (1808-1887), an American political philosopher, individualist and anarchist.

> If justice be not a natural principle, governments (so-called) have no more right or reason to take cognizance of it, or to pretend or profess to take cognizance of it, than they have to take cognizance, or to pretend or profess to take cognizance, of any other nonentity; and all their professions of establishing justice, or of maintaining justice, or of regarding justice, are simply the mere gibberish of fools, or the frauds of imposters.
> —Lysander Spooner [xiv]

John Locke (1632-1704), referenced in Chapter sixteen concerning rights, is widely regarded as one of the most influential of *enlightenment thinkers,* Locke was first to postulate, that at birth the mind is a blank slate, or *tabula rasa.* In his questioning of the work of others, Locke ostensibly established the method of introspection, that of observing one's emotions, and behaviour.

Sir William Blackstone (1723-1780) an English jurist, judge, and Tory politician, also deserves mention. Noted for his controversial legacy, the main work of which are his *Commentaries,* it is said that had they not been written when they were, likely the United States, and other English-speaking countries, would not have adopted the common law.

> Those rights, then, which God and nature have established, and are therefore called natural rights, such as life and liberty, need not the aid of human laws to be more effectually invested in every man than they are; neither do they receive any additional strength when declared by the municipal laws to be inviolate. On the contrary, no human legislature has power to abridge or destroy them, unless the owner shall himself commit some act that amounts to a forfeiture. — Sir William Blackstone [xv]

Restoration of natural order

It becomes plainly evident, that two opposing trains of thought have run parallel throughout much of human history. Expressed differently, a radically different view, from that which prevails, is available to those who seek it. Continuing from where Spencer and Spooner left off, recent (contemporary) authors offer a composite philosophy, concerning individuals, and natural law, amassing from their unique viewpoints.

- **Ludwig von Mises:** (1881-1973) Mises was the acknowledged leader of the Austrian School of economic thought. His principle view, proffered that the issue is always the same, government or the market, with no third solution. A prodigious originator in economic theory, and a prolific author, Mises's writings and lectures encompassed economic theory, history, epistemology, government, and political philosophy.
- **Ayn Rand:** (1905 - 1982) Her best-known work, the novel *Atlas Shrugged*, 1957, offered her philosophy of *objectivism* to the world. In advocating reason, as the only means of acquiring knowledge, Rand supported rational and ethical egoism, condemning the initiation of force as immoral. Opposed to collectivism, and statism, including anarchism, she instead supported laissez-faire capitalism, based on upholding

individual rights. Highly critical of most philosophical traditions, she nonetheless found some agreements with Aristotle, Thomas Aquinas, and classical liberals.

- **Murray Rothbard:** (1926-1995) Rothbard was the founder and leading theoretician of anarcho-capitalism, and staunch advocate of historical revisionism. His contribution to twentieth-century American libertarian movement is noteworthy, underscored by over twenty books on political theory, revisionist history, economics, and other subjects. His view, that services provided by the *'monopoly system of the corporate state'* be more efficiently provided by the private sector, concurs with mine. The state, he argued, is *'the organisation of robbery systematised and writ large.'*
- **Frank van Dun:** (1947-) is a Belgian law philosopher, and libertarian natural law theorist. A subscriber of private law society, or anarcho-capitalism, Van Dun argues that every natural person (individual) has a lawful claim on his life, freedom, and property. Moreover, this claim is absolute, provided it does not prohibit equivalent claims of other natural persons, insofar as argumentation is respected. Van Dun clearly distinguishes the lawful (ius) from the legal (lex). Arguing that correct interpretation of the non-aggression principle (NAP) is praxeological, rather than physical, his offerings on *natural law vs the legal*, and *Kritarchy*, are indispensable to any student of jurisprudence.

Other contributors of note, all accessible on the internet include Larken Rose (*Most Dangerous Superstition*), Craig Biddle (theobjectivestandard.com) and James A Donald (constitution.org). Not all address natural law directly, nonetheless their particular views support it. Caution urges distinction between *divine, secular* and *historical natural law.* (For explanation of the differences please refer to http://legal-dictionary.thefreedictionary.com/natural+law)

The general principle of justice

For any theory, and practice of natural law, it is imperative to distinguish between innocent individuals and those who are not innocent. Justness, is served by one who is innocent, one who is acting within the natural law. Conversely, those who elect to violate natural law, have chosen to be outlaws. They are not innocent of their actions.

The difference between *justness* and *justice* is that—

- **Justness,** manifests one's moral choice of action.
- **Justice,** is exercised to remediate unjust actions; those that are immoral.

Natural justice is lawful restoration or remediation of the (just) natural order.

- Its general principle is that— *only innocent individuals (persons) are free.*
- Its objective principle is *to act within the natural law.*

One found guilty of injustice, cannot justly be considered to be a free individual belonging only to him or herself. By his or her action, proper justice is acquired by the victim. The victim has just right to remedial measures, and or recompense, in restoration of the natural order, that (correctly) should have prior applied. Stated differently; whosoever victimises another living human being, so violating his/her rights, including property, voluntarily gives up their personal rights. So it now belongs by right to his/her victim(s), for the purpose of correcting, or remediating wrongdoing, and or recompensing the victim. Further, this power remains until that action, or aggression, is restoratively closed.

That is the general principle of Natural Justice according to natural law.

> One's actions, in violation of the individual rights of another, constitutes their unspoken consent for natural justice to be administered in (full) measure of their trespass.

—Max Emmons Taylor Jr, US-WI-2-460613-0629-1

How simple is that?

> The primary practical objective, of the juristic study of Natural Law, is to propose rules or practical principles that, if followed by human beings, are likely to maintain, strengthen and restore respect for the natural order of the human world. They are the principles and rules of justice. —Frank van Dun [14]

Moral justness invokes the personal need to be accountable for one's actions, including acceptance of justice measures. Van Dun continues—

> That does not mean the requirements of justice are contradictory. A person who inadvertently or in a temporary fit violates the Natural Law can always volunteer to undo his transgression or to submit to a procedure of arbitration to determine the kind and amount of restitution he owes to another. No violent action against such a tort-feasor is necessary. —Frank van Dun [14]

Those principles have no correlation with (today's) collective justice, positive law, legal justice, or any variant thereof. So-called justice that serves the state, or any form of collective morality, is morally bereft from its conception; capable of nothing but injustice, in theory and practice.

From an educational standpoint, the practical objective of the student of natural law, is to instil respect for that order of freedom among likes; to instil the sense and practice of justness. Nonetheless, powerful and influential individuals, groups or organisations may find, that applying justness hinders the realisation of their projects. They will show no respect for natural laws that outlaw their corrupt practices, presently hidden behind what most believe is morally or legally acceptable.

The truth remains, however.

- **Justness** is (first) served by each man and woman, not interfering with, or forbidding any other person their ability to live and sustain their life.
- **Justice** is (secondarily) served to each offender, as a correction, remediation, repatriation or restoration, in the measure of their offence. The tool of justice is correction, not punishment.

Justice, is not concerned with the intent of an action committed by one against another, but by the unjustness of one, forcibly preventing another from living his or her life, and or use of his or her property. Justice is concerned with the forcible removal of such stoppage, and restoration of the natural order. That is all.

Natural justice

To quote Van Dun, *'Justice is for mature adults who are supposed to know the difference between the real world and the games people play.'* Justice corrects unjustness. The role of natural justice, is to steer offenders back to an ethic based morality, moral congruence, and acceptance of others right to life. Is recompense involved? Yes, in many cases, although mitigating circumstances may prevail. Note that because no victimless crime can exist, no penalty, remedy or restitution can be levied.

Natural justice, as a practice, is for a *Commission of Justice*. Forbidden to make rules or laws, its role is to determine whether another's rights have been violated, based on the *Constitution of Man*, (Chapter 22), and if so, to institute remedy, and or restitution, according to the measure, and permission, (prior) chosen by the convicted offender.

Natural law is the only foundation, for a convivial (congenial) order of natural living persons. Conditions of conviviality are objective, and universal, the same at all times and places, in any human population. Natural law upholding moral justness for all individuals, stands in opposition to any social order founded on artificial persons, legalities, or positive law.

21

SYMBIOTIC SOCIETY

Who, today, has lived without government authority? We know nothing different, because we've never challenged statism, or its legal, and (purported) moral authority. We've so little understood who and what we truly are, and that all social intercourse is properly individual, before it is communal.

Society by Company, corporatised government, has known from inception that its criminal conduct could only succeed, first, while citizens remain ignorant of its counterfeit methods, and second, while living men and women remain convinced, that collective society must rule over Mans individuality.

Fully practised, mistaken ideologies, have allowed governments to conceal evil, while denying or refuting everything that might reveal it. Few know that governments are little more than criminal syndicates in principle, profiting from deliberate perversion, effectively upholding murder of Man's soul.

There is an alternative. That is to allow and encourage a *symbiotic society*. To fully understand this option, is to adopt a very different mindset. It means the abandonment of ruling society, and instituting one that never will. That mindset is centuries overdue.

Natural law invites life

Man is not impelled to any particular social order, but will naturally gravitate to organic sociability characterised by convivial association, that is friendly, lively, and enjoyable. These attitudes imply and impart equal standing, mutual respect, cooperation and collaboration, in all societal or business interactions; all in their (individual) approach, their action, and in their separation.

The founding premise is that Man is (socially) spiritual, not animal, or fundamentally materialistic.

We're all taught that morality must be ruled, which, as explained above, is why the mindset of *rule* survives any challenge. Further, why would we question that basis of morality, when it ostensibly offers comforts and protections? So we have morally accepted that one man, or woman, may rule others.

Creator's alternative awaits. Natural law invites life. Natural law is constructive, supportive, gracious, purposeful, loving, and spiritually uplifting; authority, rule, and initiated force are nowhere found! Tables turn unmistakably. When transgressors self-confess need for remediation by their actions, free people need no commandments but their own morality. It follows that education concerning morality, law, and justice, is overdue serious revision.

Participants of an organic, symbiotic society, come together as equals for a mutual uncoerced benefit, else they go separately as they came. Freedom pertains only to single persons. The word *freedom* does not apply to society, or any public realm. Liberty is the (proper) *collective term* applicable to a community. To be free, means living beings, free in mind, and spirit, no exceptions; fully independent from all legal or fictional persons, citizens, or Legal Entities. Free individuals have the capacity, and immutable right to act in support of their life, according to free choice, this capacity remaining until death. To destroy real freedom, one has to kill the individual.

Consider these—

- Organic society is symbiotic. It is of free, independent people, living according to their choices among their likes. They respect the natural law of the human world, in their mutual dealings and interactions. Its convivial order, is that of adults living as responsible and caring people.
- Such convivial society is the meeting, exchanging, and parting, or of freely entering into, or exiting from more or less durable relationships, on peaceful and friendly terms within a good will atmosphere.
- All people are free to the extent that others treat them peacefully, with friendliness and respect, also respecting their rights, their work, and their property. It is this mutual respect, one for another, within the physical domain of which they are the author, that all interactions accord with *ius*; meaning *natural law*.
- People live together as independent beings, without being impelled to any common enterprise or social interaction, not unlike a commune.
- Friendly relations among strangers, having nothing but their humanity in common, are natural to their nature, while offering due respect for other's uniqueness, individuality, personal integrity and property.
- Natural laws discovered within, preserve individuality, and individual rights, not *rights* which are really permissions, written by Man.
- Individual freedom allows opportunity, facilitates negotiations, actions, and outcomes, yet allows free exit, all absent force, fraud, or coercion.
- Individuals are free to lawfully pursue their own goals, separately, in the company of, or in collaboration with others. Business contracts are personally and responsibly warranted, not committed by office, title, position, company, or corporation.

- Such convivial symbiotic order, has no organisational, or statutory purpose. It has no leader, director, or governor, neither owners.
- Nothing in organic society establishes rulers, or the ruled. No individual, or group owns it, rules it, is responsible or answerable for it. No common goal exists, neither does any central authority control or direct activities of the people in it.
- No authority exercise direction, rule, or control, meaning no government may exist, because such forfeits the nature, and integrity, of an organic, symbiotic society's very existence.
- Relationships of direction, and influence may exist in the convivial order, e.g., from elders and those of great wisdom, but there are no positions of power to exert influence, or command.
- Participants abide the natural laws of its orderliness. Natural law ethics, clearly differs from judgements of justice (moral).
- Those who choose to step outside natural laws, have chosen to be outlaws, and by their actions, agree to suffer all consequences arising.
- The arrest of violence, and service of natural justice, remediation, and recompense, accords with natural law.
- All problems are resolved by diplomatic negotiations, or by appointing a judge, or arbitrator, always remembering, that no one who seeks resolution can become the subject of the negotiator, or any judicial agent.
- No convivial organic order can wage war!

Society of this kind, cannot be the driving force of Mankind. In total contrast, to diagrams illustrating government, shown in Chapter 1, here diagram 15 illustrates a symbiotic society in principle. There is no government, yet people's right to life is upheld, and protected. Outlaws are dealt with by the *Commission of Justice*, that cannot make any laws. Its reference base is the *'laws of nature and nature's God,'* exactly as Thomas Jefferson wrote in the 1776 *Declaration of Independence*. These, as this work has shown, are indelibly written within each of us, so that they cannot be repealed, revised or re-written.

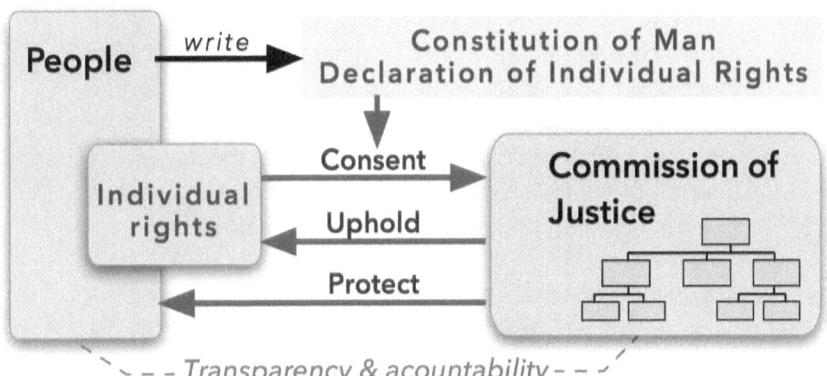

15 - Symbiotic society

Observe that the *Commission of Justice* has only two functions; to uphold individual rights, and protect the people. It has only one entry point, namely the individual rights of the people. Should it fail its task, people have the right to abolish it, and begin over. It is servant of the populace, as individuals, not vice versa as governments are today.

Individual participants are the sole source of purposive action, not any structure they may have instituted to protect their right to actions, and property. To be free, is to be independently active and to exist by one's efforts. One is his or her own, one's mind is his or her own, one's life is his or her own. One's efforts are one's own. No one may rule conversely. Others are free in like manner, to live their life, and make their personal decisions.

Agorism and Kritarchy

Symbiotic society, as described above, is neither *agorism* or a *kritarchy*, but closely resembles both. Agorism usually embraces counter-economics, however, that concern is more tactical than philosophical. Omit economics, and *agorism* more closely approximates *kritarchy*.

Although this is commonly defined as *'a system of rule by judges,'* dig deeper, and a different meaning presents.

> Kritarchy is the political system based on equal justice for all, which is to say on respect for natural law. It differs from other political systems by its consistent adherence to and application of the rules of justice. Even courts of law, police forces and other organisations that look after the day-to-day business of maintaining law, are denied any power, privilege or immunity that is not in conformity with natural law.
>
> A kritarchy does not know the usual political distinction between subjects and rulers. It lacks a government in the modern sense of the word, i.e. an organisation with coercive powers that claims a right to the obedience or to the use of the labour or the property of those who inhabit or reside in the area over which its coercive powers are effective. — Frank van Dun [xvi]

It is too easy to be enamoured by names. Anarchy, voluntarism, libertarianism, agorism, minarchy, and kritarchy, all espouse the same thing in broad principle. The name is unimportant. Freedom to live according to natural law is not.

Tyrannical domination and control bind Man today. Our focus should be, to discover and implement what life properly should be without it.

Ius versus Lex.

Natural law, as *invitation,* differs markedly from *law,* as *rule.* Yet, sadly, it is often accepted that even in natural law, the word *law* stands for a command, a *rule,* executive order, or some directive statement. Accordingly, most folks interpret that a law commands, permits that something be done, or forbids it being done.

Law as instruction, originates from the translation of the Latin word *'lex.'* A *lex,* in the general sense, means a contract, usually written. Its original meaning, and use, came from the mobilisation of armies, and the organising of military campaigns. The word *lex*, derives from the Latin root verb, *ligare*, 'to bind.' Progressively, over years, Lex came to mean any general directive, rule, or law issued by the highest political authorities.

Have we been misled? Yes, reason being that the word *law*, was also used to translate the Latin word *'Ius'*. 'Ius,' ('*iurare*', to swear), refers to a bond or obligation that arises out of a personal commitment made in a solemn speech. More generally *Ius* denotes an order of human affairs, stemming from such mutual commitment. Differently, *ius* can mean a natural, or customary right. Accordingly, an *ius* can exist, without it being codified, thus making it independent of written law.

The overall outcome is ambiguous. If Lex means a contract, usually written as law, and Ius can mean a natural or customary right, independent of written law, then Lex and Ius are very different, if not opposed.

So what term, might give *law*, natural standing? The answer is, that the word *lex*, becomes *'Lex Naturale,'* or *'Lex Naturalis.'* Although these terms are said to be *natural law*, the concept of *rule* remains attached, from its lex origin. Ambiguity arises, because, whereas *Lex Naturale* combines legal provision, as law, supposedly with a natural right granted by it, *Ius* has nothing to do with exercising political authority.

Readers are urged discernment, for much spoken of today concerning *natural law,* refers to *Lex Naturalis,* not *Ius Naturalis,* despite that both are generically referred to as *natural law*. Effectively, *Lex* seeks a natural *permission* for authority to rule. The fact that true natural law is *invitation*, not *command*, is why I included the term *Ius Naturalis* on the cover of this book. *Ius Naturalis* stands in vivid contrast to *Lex Naturalis,* that permits that one man, or woman, can unilaterally oblige or rule another.

Ius upholds conditions wherein people meet as free and equal individuals, permitting arrangement of their affairs by agreement, contracts or covenants. Look again at the natural laws described here, and they all point to such a society.

Productive society

Three great values gained from a convivial social existence are peace, knowledge and trade.

Because Man is the only living species that can share, and expand his knowledge from one generation to the next, growth of knowledge potentially available to each, is greater than any one individual could begin to acquire in his/her lifespan. Every man and woman on earth stand to gain incalculable benefit, from the knowledge discovered by others.

Rewarding and life-sustaining facilitations are not automatic. They must be diligently sought after, worked at, accorded respect for their truthfulness, authenticity, and safe efficiency. Actions indicate, delimit and define what kind of Men can be of value to one another—every man and woman free to cultivate beneficial, or detrimental outcomes of their actions, all free to learn of consequences prior.

Knowledge and free trade in an independently based, rational, productive, and free society will positively benefit. Such does not mean that those of lesser ability will miss out. To the contrary, most often, those less capable are the greatest beneficiaries of freedom and unfettered production.

> Spain is without a national government and the people are loving it. For over 280 days, the Spanish people have been without an elected government and, as it seems, it is the greatest thing to have happened to the country since it's four-decades-old democracy began. In the words of language teacher, Félix Pastor, "no government, no thieves." Though the leaders warned that the country without a government would fall into chaos, the opposite seems to have happened.

Since officials have stepped out of the way, people are thriving. —Secrets of the fed.[xvii]

Parasites, moochers, looters, second-handers, bullies, pirates, thugs, even corporate governments, offer no value to any individual in convivial society. Neither can such poachers gain any benefit from a society geared to freely satisfying needs and life-sustaining actions, precisely because their criminal actions plunder the very benefits they wish to obtain.

No government can exist in an organic, convivial society—nothing exists to give it an unfair advantage, pander stupidity, insolence, arrogance or bloody-minded criminality.

Division of labour, in an organic society, enables each to devote his/her effort to a particular field of work, thence, to trade with others working in other areas. Cooperation allows that all who take part can achieve greater knowledge, skill, and productive return on their effort, than they could make alone.

Governments also thrive on the division of labour, yours and mine, however, because their focus is regulation, not production, so parasitism grows in advance of it. Bankers, war profiteers, and drug dealers are parasites, equally as thieves, slackers and second-handers who contribute nothing. They utterly rely on your production, and mine, and will fight like cornered rats to enslave you.

Before 1913, Americans kept 100% of their pay cheque, but still there were roads, schools, colleges, and fire departments. Peace loving individuals focus on what each can do, not on what others should do, whereby division of labour makes for more choice. Those who have tasted asparagus or green beans, of their labour, also have access to tuna, theatre, transport, orchestral music, right to travel, and non-homogenised milk.

Beneficial labour division is not possible, without voluntary exchange. Without private property rights, all is expropriated; this the raw nature of (authoritative) regulatory conformity.

Independence and natural law

Unless natural law, and individual rights are given full reign, and fully protected, symbiosis will fail, as mankind's history demonstrably testifies. Some argue that convivial association can only work in low population, primitive societies, moreover that in today's high-speed, hi-tech, highly regulated society, such orderliness is wishful thinking, and highly impractical. In reply to this criticism, it must be asked what drives incessant appetite for regulation? To argue, that Man can only function when one rules over or regulates another, is to say that society can only flourish when one Man can punish another. Ruling, conformist societies, have never worked in Mans entire history, and never will they. Free production, and free uncoerced exchange, are anathema to regulation. Truth is, that the denser and more high-tech the environment, greater a free (non-ruled) society is enabled to serve it.

Any mindset, that argues Man can only function with a publicly appointed boss, president, or dictator, aided by an army of administrators, who write rules for citizens to obey while robbing them, is insane. All social and essential services, presently conducted under government aegis can, for a free society, be provided by those employed or contracted by the government today, save no public purse will excuse their ineffectiveness, inefficiency, or lack. Non-performers will be replaced by those who can, exactly as free trade has succeeded whenever it has been allowed free rein.

Josiah Warren reported concerning the *Time Store* in Cincinnati, that opened in May 1827. Symbiotic principles were applied to the management, and education of children, and to the purchase and sale of land, likewise to almost all other kinds of property, and to the interchange of labour, including that of merchants, lawyers, physicians, and teachers. Autonomy of the individual was strictly preserved at all times, and invariably respected it. No legislation, of any description, assumed control over people at any time, or for any case.

What resulted?

> Such was the complete individuality of action that hundreds dealt at the Time Store without understanding much of its principles or its objects; but they perceived that it was their interest to do so, thus demonstrating that the business of the community can be brought into this condition by a natural and irresistible process; without combination, without organisation, without laws, without government, without the surrender of any "portion" of the natural liberty of the individual; demonstrating also that reformation need not wait till the world becomes learned: but the practical operation constitutes a process of re-education which no one can estimate without experience, and which the learned are most backward in acquiring. —Josiah Warren. New Harmony, [xviii] Nov. 27, 1841. [Emphasis Mine]

Man has no need to wait longer for deliverance. Protection from aggression, is all that remains. Your freedom, respect for others, and your responsibilities, are yours alone. Your life belongs only to you, and your joy in this world, is to live it!

Protection of your rights is for a *Commission of Justice*—indeed its single address and concern. Governments, that forcefully conscript that living beings are fictional entities, are corrupt in having done so. It follows that a *Commission of Justice,* should properly be constrained to moral justice serving Mans life, and rehabilitating transgressors, never wavering from, or forsaking its special commission, or charter; else it is guilty of trespass. It cannot possibly be permitted to infringe Mans rights by rule, for that commits an injustice. Its role is severely delimited, yet granted full remedial effectiveness by the wilful actions of transgressors, or violators of Mans unalienable right to life.

Following is text offering a universal *'Constitution of Man.'* (Constructive comment and discussion is invited.)

22

CONSTITUTION OF MAN

Preamble

Mans' value has been harvested and plundered by monarchies, military rulers, dictators, lawmakers, fascist, socialist, democratic and communist regimes, tyrants, and corrupt corporations. Suffering endless tyranny, and rule for centuries, none have fully allowed the sustaining of life according to free-will choice inherent within the nature of Man, qua Man, or unalienable right to life, equally bestowed by Creator upon every Living (Homo sapiens) Being without exception. Nevertheless endowed, Independent Living Beings of planet earth now seek life, freedom, and pursuit of happiness within their unalienable natural rights, equally drawn about by the rights of all others; all authority and usurpation refused. All Independent Living Beings may fulfil their purpose, according to their choice; all initiated force, fraud, or coercion by any Independent Living Being, or group against any other forbidden, arresting force used for its cessation being lawful. To establish individual freedom, equality, and justice in perpetuity, we, the One People of Planet Earth, here ordain and establish this Constitution of Man equally of, and applicable to all Independent Living (human) Beings, in posterity, and perpetuity.

Article 1: Declaration of Individual Rights

1.1 Right to Life

1.1.1 Man's right to his own life is a self-evident truth.

1.1.2 Man's right to his own life is of nature, and by nature; natural rights are a self-evident truth.

1.1.3 Natural Rights are Unalienable Rights, belonging to every (human) Individual Living Being equally.

1.1.4 Unalienable, Individual Rights are innate, belonging to each and every Individual Living Being; indivisible further, impossible collectively.

1.1.5 Natural, Unalienable Rights of Independent Living Being's, are endowed by Creator, immutable, inviolable; neither given, taken or transferable.

1.2 Right of Equality and Sovereignty

1.2.1 All Independent Living Being's, are created equal by their Creator, by which nature of being Man, qua Man, possess equally and unequivocally the Unalienable Right to Life, permitting no trespass.

1.2.2 By the Unalienable Right to Life, endowed by Creator, all men are equally and independently sovereign, according to the equal nature of being Man, qua Man.

1.2.3 No form of eminent domain shall henceforth exist.

1.2.4 No Independent Living Being, or aggregate of Independent Living Being's, shall annul, invalidate, or usurp the unalienable rights of another. No religious claim of right, may negate or usurp the unalienable rights of any Independent Living Being.

1.2.5 No Independent Living Being, or group of Independent Living Beings, shall be legally or otherwise deemed, classified, or treated as animal.

1.2.6 Independent Rights of Man, preside over all other life forms.

1.3 Right to Liberty

1.3.1 Life, Freedom, and the Pursuit of Happiness, are the Unalienable Right(s) of every Independent Living Being.

1.3.2 Free-will choice of thought and action, by any and all Independent Living Being's, are guaranteed inclusive of the responsibility, liability and accountability, naturally, and inherently flowing therefrom.

1.3.3 No Living Being severally, or Independent Living Being's collectively, may initiate force, coercion, blackmail, or fraud against any Independent Living Being's self, or property.

1.4 Right to Value and Property

1.4.1 Unalienable rights, immutably inherent in the natural essence of Man are: they cannot form, or be the object of a transaction, or contractual agreement, whether voluntary,, or involuntary.

1.4.2 Individual property rights, derive from every Independent Living Being's Unalienable Right to action; from which action, material property is cultivated, made, or earned.

1.4.4 Any Independent Living Being's lawful action, that removes from the state of nature, and that blends his or her labour with material matter, to his or her enhancement of life, over that which has no owner, constitutes his, or her, inalienable right to the product/property thereby cultivated, made,, or earned.

1.4.5 Property exchange transfers rights over things, but it does not create the right.

1.4.6 Unalienable Rights, are fully preserved in any process to contract for the acquisition, transfer, or exchange of property.

1.4.7 Each Independent Living Being, has the right to own personal property, free and clear of all encumbrances. No right to alienate property rights over things, entails the right to alienate the right itself, property rights thus preserved.

1.4.8 Value, resulting from each and every Independent Living Being's thought, speech, and action to cultivate, make, earn or exchange property, is guaranteed, including each Independent Living Being's free will choice to gift, trade, or dispose of his or her value, or property.

1.4.9 No redistribution of wealth, using legislative assemblies or any such-like institution, shall ever exist, unless by/for the reparation of crimes committed against another.

1.4.10 Property, being that which can be gifted, bought, or sold, is alienable, but the acquisition of property ownership by any other means, violates clause 1.4.7 of this *Constitution of Man*.

1.5 Right of Abdication

1.5.1 By the nature of Man, qua Man, whosoever violates, denies, or abrogates the rights of another, does by that action, abdicate the free-will right to so choose.

1.5.2 Save to protect the life of another Independent Living Being, initiation of force against another, constitutes the wilful surrender of self-rights for that duration, for which no mitigating circumstance may prevail.

1.5.3 Every Independent Living Being, has the Unalienable Right to dispose fully and freely of one's own body (life), of one's own faculties, of the fruits of one's labours, in non-violation of the rights of others.

1.6 Right of Independence

1.6.1 Any living being attaining the age of fifteen (15) years, may until age eighteen, subject to clause 1.6.3, choose to accept, hold and honour a "Probationary Acceptance (of) Sovereignty Status," (hereafter PASS), such PASS redundant attaining age eighteen years.

1.6.2 PASS holders choose by this means to accept the *Age of Independence*, and abiding by their sovereignty, to fully uphold the *Declaration of Individual Rights*, the *Constitution of Man*, with full responsibility, and accountability, for their actions thereafter.

1.6.3 Any PASS holder, found to have transgressed their rights, and to have violated the *Declaration of Individual Rights*, and or this *Constitution of Man,* shall be held fully accountable for their actions as though adult, and by prior agreement in accepting a PASS, forfeit adult sovereign status until attaining the age of eighteen years.

1.6.4 Any PASS holder, who, having held a PASS for twenty-four months, without violation or abrogation of another's rights, may claim full adult sovereignty, though aged less than eighteen years.

1.7 Right of Protection

1.7.1 Retaliatory force may lawfully, and morally be used, by any living being separately, or Independent Living Beings collectively, only in defence against those who violate Clauses 1.1 through 1.4 inclusive herein;

1.7.2 Physical retaliatory force, is lawfully limited to that necessary to arrest or cause force initiated against Independent Living Being's self, or property, to cease. (Refer to Article 4)

1.8 Rights in Perpetuity

1.8.1 By the right to life, in-bodied by all Independent Living Being's, including value derived therefrom, no living being separately, or Individuals collectively, shall abrogate, subjugate, subordinate, fraudulently acquire, usurp, blackmail, invade, violate, commandeer, steal, arrest, confiscate, or detain the duly secured value of life, or property, by principle of Natural Law of any Independent Living Being's domicil, without prejudice, by creation, on earth.

1.9 Exceptions

1.9.1 No exception shall ever exist or amendment be made to Clauses 1 through 7 herein, inclusive.

Article 2: Group Rights

2.1 Group Rights

2.1.1 No rights are ascribed, or conferred to 'collective' bodies; aggregate numbers of Individual Living Beings regardless of howsoever claimed.

2.1.2 Conglomerate, (whole) sums of Individual Living Beings, can have no rights they do not as Individual Living Beings, already possess.

2.1.3 Human rights, indigenous rights, fundamental rights, workers rights, or other such claimed 'collective rights' are obsolete; redundant.

Article 3: Previous laws

3.1 Previous laws Null and Void

3.1.1 This *Constitution of Man,* for any state, or country that adopts it, henceforth supersedes, overrides, and makes null and void all current laws, positive law, regulations, directives, statutes, or executive orders that, now or in the past, conflict with any part of this *Constitution of Man*, in that State, Country, or Jurisdiction, regardless of previous or current authority, save Creator's natural laws.

3.1.2 This *Constitution of Man,* offered as Global, and Universal Republic, by express *Declaration of Individual Rights* inherent in man, qua man, under the rule of Natural Law, expressly denies all forms of tyrannical rule, howsoever quantified, or constructed, including that known as 'Democracy'.

3.1.3 No form of 'legal fiction,' or legal 'personification,' pertaining to any Individual Living Being, howsoever named, described, or legislated shall henceforth exist.

Article 4: Protection

4.1 Commission for One People's Protection

4.1.1 By the *Declaration of Individual Rights*, independence, and freedom thus established, the aggregate sum of

Individual Living Beings that are 'One People,' now seek unto themselves an elected body commissioned to protect every Individual Living Being's Right to Life, as set out in this document. Wherefrom is secured, and guaranteed, rightful freedom to unobstructed action according to One's will, within limits drawn around each by the equal unalienable rights of all other Independent Living Beings

4.1.2 This elected body, including all branches, shall be known as the *Commission of Justice* its purpose to equally uphold, and protect sovereign, unalienable, individual rights, of all members of society, for orderly, universal, peaceful, harmonious co-existence of human life.

4.1.3 This *Commission of Justice*, including all branches chartered as *Regional Commissions of Justice,* shall each have jurisdiction in and over a land mass, which area is agreed by the One People, (hereafter jurisdiction).

4.1.4 These various societies, shall share common jurisdiction overlap, so to protect Individual Rights fluidly and equally, in common, as though one homogenous jurisdiction, regardless of culture, race, ethnicity, beliefs, or island, country, continent, hemisphere or planet; *One People.*

4.1.5 Each separate *Regional Commission of Justice,* is fully bound by this *Constitution of Man,* to conform to the "Charter" for the *Regional Commission of Justice.*

4.1.6 By this *Constitution of Man,* each separate *Regional Commission of Justice,* is expressly forbidden any alternative intent, or control, in any jurisdiction, including but not limited to any law, rule, regulation, statute, directive, or executive order, for so long as Man is Man (in perpetuity). Neither is permitted any construct, amendment, alteration, addition, abuse, or misuse of words in this document, that might or would violate any article of this *Constitution of Man.*

4.1.7 No *Independent Commission of Justice* may offer, or provide protection, as described in the "Charter" for the *Regional Commission of Justice,* in or by any corporation, commercial, or business manner.

Article 5: Commission of Justice

5.1 Grant of Charter: Independent Commission of Justice

5.1.1 This *Constitution of Man,* hereby issues a *Grant of Charter* for the establishment and maintenance of an *Individual Commission of Justice,* whose purpose and function is to uphold this *Constitution of Man* in accordance with Creator's Natural Laws.

5.1.2 By this Grant of Charter, all *Independent Commissions of Justice's* so established, shall—

   a) uphold the *Declaration of Individual Rights* as specified in Article 1 of this *Constitution of Man;*

   b) do that necessary to preserve Individual Rights as specified in Article 1 of this *Constitution of Man,* through sub-structures of the *Independent Commissions of Justice* known as Police Commission, Judiciary Commission, and Support Commission.

Article 6: Amendments

6.1 Amendments to this Constitution of Man

6.1.1 No Article, or Section thereof, of this *Constitution of Man,* shall ever be repealed or abrogated in whole or part.

23

THE LESSON

When (Creator's) natural laws that govern Man's nature, are correctly instituted to enable a just society, so are the means to keep it.

Save for some remote tribes; such a free, convivial society has never before existed. Once established, it would make redundant every government that has ever existed, absolve and eliminate all victimless crime, cancel all legality, and authority, institute freedom, justness, and justice, all founded of the nature and life of individual living men, and women.

That is not a big task, for two reasons.

1. Maintaining today's governments is a monumental task, by comparison. Government workers could find productive jobs.
2. A *Commission of Justice,* could easily employ those who presently work in law, and justice, provided they can mentally transit to serving freedom, instead of corporate interests. The same applies to police administrators, and employees.

The question is; should we learn how, and why domination and control have succeeded for millennia without challenge, or, focus on how natural law can overthrow it? The correct answer is both.

Greatest emphasis should be given to Man's *life*, as inescapable truth, the remainder teaching how to avoid misuse of this knowledge.

Education Factors

This book has posed many viewpoints that differ from common acceptance, some more vital than others, but all important nonetheless. Let's view their totality.

1. EXISTENCE: The fact that *existence precedes consciousness* is indisputable. Life must exist before any cognitive understanding of it, and that order is irreversible. Creator's natural laws of identity, and causality, preclude it—or consciousness is a lie. Many philosophies, ideologies, and theologies such as mysticism, collectivism, subjectivism, altruism, and (government) statism thrive on this lie. Governments will fight tooth and nail to reverse, subvert, or fictionally replace Mans nature, never grasping that impossibility; never admitting that to maintain/uphold/enforce lies, that defy one's nature, is to spit in Creator's face.
2. BELIEFS: Blend conscious, and subconscious mind processes together, as though one, and bogus ideologies may quickly be assimilated as truth. Abandon enquiry, investigation, and validation, and undesirable outcomes are entirely predictable. Notions invented by others will then assume authority, necessarily enforced, because all disagreement is considered unethical, immoral, or both. Free will is thereby overruled, and authority presides, ostensibly because Man has a *'tendency to evil.'* No protest is possible; investigation, validation, and truth long abandoned. Morality assumes a collective prerogative, that everyone is beguiled to believe.
3. ERRANT IDEOLOGY: When societal laws invented by Man, take root, because seemingly that's all there is, the result is entirely predictable. No valid checkpoint exists; all is subjective. Cause traces from bogus philosophies, theologies, and ideologies, all based on consciousness as the (subjective)

arbiter of existent reality. Join those dots, and Man must be consciously governed by an *authority,* as unchallengeable necessity. Some non-thinking, or agenda-driven individual declared Man a *social animal,* and since, no one has ever questioned the validity of such an asinine assertion. Nothing will change while subjective ideology rules.

4. DECEPTION: Perception is always truthful. For animals, no investigation is possible. For Man, it induces thought, whereby understanding may be false, or misguided.

5. Once convinced that *awareness* means *understanding,* how easy would it be to persuade Man that the state is legitimately truthful, and that no investigation is warranted, or even possible.

6. Does this explain how tyrants protect themselves—how they capitalise false ideologies that subvert real concepts, and how they use the *social animal* concept to forge universal acceptance of top-down control, in all cultures and countries, thereby crushing all investigation into (their) state criminality?

7. CONSENT: That you are an independent living being, is fact. It is also fact that you are regarded as a *citizen;* a fictional legal entity, a *natural person,* subject to statute laws backed by force. Government necessarily relies on you actuating your legal entity; else its fraudulent creation, would remain the dead fiction that it is. Fictional entities cannot open letters, read, write, speak, cook, or drive. So you must apply, register, present, be licensed, vote, conform, and submit to every (applicable) rule of authority government makes; every statute it says is law; because without your participation, as its *legal servant,* it has nothing.

8. *Consent of the governed,* initially meant assured protection of one's life. No more; consent now means to forgo life's value, by submitting to authority and obeying its every command.

9. LAW: Government administered *positive law* (legally) countermands *natural law,* and cannot do otherwise. If government upheld the natural law, then no need would exist for any other. While ever rule over Man is enacted,

Mans right to life is canceled. Freedom to live, and freedom to rule Man, are antithetical. That which assumes supremacy, outlaws the other, this the crossroad Man's conscious mind now faces.

10. EVIL: Some people do err; some do commit acts of evil, but their actions are of their free choice, not a tendency. To conclude that Man has a *tendency to evil,* and impress this upon Man as truth so as to justify authority, and rule enforcement, is to contradict, or deny Mans free will nature. A biased will is not free.

11. FORCED ANIMALITY: Man's chosen refusal to engage in cognitive understanding, forces him to function in a state akin to animality—to depend entirely on his automatic processes. Full automation cannot be, because Man is not so equipped! Moreover, governments force Man to adapt to state laws, similar to the manner by which animals adjust to nature. So the state forces Man to function in a state akin to animality; forces reliance on the mechanics of legalities, and the state; compels he obey the edicts of another.

12. RIGHT TO LIFE: One's right to life is individual, because one's life is indisputably one's own being; not property. Because no collective liver, brain, or stomach exists, so no group rights can exist; despite the (1948) UDHR document. Unless a government upholds individual rights, then whatever rights it portends to support are imaginary; permissions based on the rejection of natural law, and every individual's right to life.

13. PERCEPTION: Perception is fuel for our conscious mind, that prompts free will to think. Understanding is vastly different. The first is automatic, and the second is of choice. When the legitimate phrase *conscious awareness* is considered to mean *conscious understanding,* beliefs so easily become synonymous with knowledge, whereby Man is easily misled, while firmly convinced he is knowledgeable.

14. INDIVIDUALITY: Every man, and woman, is a singular being of creation. The notion held in psychology of *family* being the smallest unit of society, is plainly false; core tenet

of subjectivism, collectivism, and the founding premise of statism.

15. FREE WILL: Freedom to think, means not surrendering the sovereignty of one's mind to anyone, any belief, or any other. Nothing serves one's thought, one's knowledge, or self-mastery, when rulers, neighbours, or imposters are the term-setters of one's mind. Free will is not free license to act, irrespective of consequence. It encompasses one's responsibility *towards* others; but not one's responsibility *for* them. Unceasing respect for the lives of others, is the only means by which to guarantee one's freedom!

16. PROCESS vs. CONTENT: Mans free choice as to what he will think, and the process of thinking, are two different things. *Mental process*, as distinct from *mental content*, ranks near the top, considering life's vital importance, yet receives little or no attention in social, and human sciences. Witness that Man agrees that he can *change his mind*, but *never influence his subconscious mind*, and you'll see how social, and human sciences, have failed to express the truth of Man's life on two counts. Left in a vacuum, not of his making, Man readily falls prey to every salvation, particularly when truth is less important than fast relief from emotional distress.

17. MENTORING: Given that our chosen values program our subconscious mind, emotions objectively inform whether our values are being upheld or hindered. Absent subsequent investigation they establish nothing. Never before described, as a mentoring system, the role of free will respective of conscience, and emotions, hails a complete overhaul of human science.

18. VOCABULARY: Whereas the language, or vocabulary of the conscious mind is word concepts; subconscious mind uses an image vocabulary. For data to pass from conscious to the subconscious mind, it must first be transmitted in the vocabulary by which it will be received, and understood. This transference helps to explain surreptitious mind controls methods, and the vital need for intellectual integrity.

19. OBJECTIVITY: Great difference exists between (objectively) knowing, and (subjectively) believing. It is the difference between fact and fiction, life or death, morality and morality, justness versus unjustness. Truth does not allow for knowledge, fact, life, morality and justness, to be bent to some one's personal, or political persuasion. The *natural laws of identity* and *causality* forbid it. It is for that reason exactly, that fictional ideas, or notions, are invented and impressed on the minds of Man as truth. Nonetheless, truth and falsity always remain distinguishable. Man's nature obliges that he learn the difference.

20. EDUCATION: Literature concerning Man's six higher senses fails to distinguish between *conscious* and *subconscious* processes, much less their sequential orderliness. The automatic process must separate from free will process, else (governing) natural laws are concealed, thereby omitted from consideration. Man is obliged to adapt to prevailing consensus, or authoritarian rule, because natural laws seemingly do not exist. Education concerning ethics, and morality, needs overhaul, likewise human sciences dealing with conscious mind, subconscious mind, emotions, and Mans six higher faculties. Ethics can be included and made a core underwriting of most disciplines. Consistency is more important than content, meaning that the subject of ethics should underscore different curricular, not swamp it.

21. JUSTICE: Because one's choice to act switches from (thought) ethics, to (actioned) morality, moral, or immoral actions, are divorced from ethical, or non-ethical thinking, that gave rise to them. Justice is concerned only with remediating wrongful actions thereby; not the correction of wrong thinking. That is a pre-emptive task for human science education.

22. SPIRITUALITY: Consciously, or unconsciously, we choose spiritual values that we desire physical enactments should bring us. Two-way communion, and communication between our conscious and subconscious mind, are a value-based spiritual exchange. Thus we are *spiritual beings,* living

a *spiritual life*, served by an existent reality that we adapt to our purposes.

Man's nature, should properly be the central point of human and social sciences, therefore. Focus should not so much be our free will actions, rather the entirety of all evaluative process. This forms the science of Ethics. All of the above may seem intense, or involved to some folk, but it is not. All reduce to simple principles. When reiterated consistently, and regularly, they each will afford ample opportunities for more detailed explanations and wider understanding.

Ethics and Morality

Many consider *ethics,* to be moral principles governing a person's behaviour, or activity, that determines the moral correctness of (a specified) action.

Why can't we just accept this simplicity, and not confuse it? Why do so many people confuse what is right or wrong in terms of their own life, with religious beliefs, what the law requires, or standards of behaviour that society determines to be acceptable? These folks don't know that ethics, and morality, are personal matters. They firmly believe that others should set moral standards. They cannot mentally connect cause with effect. They cannot see that it is they who determine the moral correctness of their conduct, not rulers, or religious leaders. So the meaning of morality has been usurped; translated to mean that society, church, or the collective will determine ethics, and morality, and that your behaviour must conform to their edicts. So it is that morality has nothing to do with what is right for an individual; instead, opinions or preferences coercively imposed upon others.

Consequently, many people are confused. They feel bound to act according to what they consider is moral, yet feel compelled to follow what others believe is right, never realising, that while the state claims moral status, it creates and masterminds tyranny, which is immoral.

The state exercises moral authority with widespread approval, including its enforcement. Sadly, these folk have no understanding of natural laws, inherent within them, or that (principled) ethical thoughts, occasion moral actions, whereby feelings follow. They've no understanding of how their mental processes work in sequence, to uphold their life, or how *ethics* traces from the natural laws of one processes, and faculties. They don't know, because natural law is shunted aside, as though it never existed.

Consider this. If self professed leaders, are able to convince Man that morality is a social necessity to be administered by church, or state, then they have considerable influence over Man's thoughts. They know the ropes, they're the leaders, others are ignorant sheeple. Man has been devastatingly indoctrinated, to believe in authoritarian rule, and his personal insignificance in the face of it, for far too long. If these *leaders,* then enforce that certain actions must conform to their societal prescription, what do they now hold in their hands? Thoughts, actions, or both? Power is the right answer. Does that explain, why you're indoctrinated to abide societal conformity? Religious, and secular leaders, fully intend you should be kept ignorant of the fact that ethics, and morality, concern your individual life, else you would not willingly sacrifice your life to their edicts.

How will Man know that he lacks vital information concerning his nature, when nothing seems to permit it, worse that he or she must be subservient to rule of the collective; not his or her own choices?

Failure of ethics, as science, cannot be more aptly stated. Fortunately, science seems to be coming to its senses as shown in several quotes given. Change is occurring. More are awakening to their sovereignty and autonomy. There is a decided turn away from globalism. It will narrow toward nationalism, then localism, eventually awakening to the wholeness of the human individual.

Then ethics may come into its own, representing the summation of one's own being, purposefully devoted to upholding his or her life. From a tender age, given that era, *ethics* will teach of choosing wisely, using right reason, logic, and efficacious integrity, congruent with the *laws of identity and causality*, in a life-supporting manner.

Focusing on the natural laws of Mans' processes, ethics should properly be an objective science, teaching Creator's personal invitation to live the fullest, most beautiful, and bountiful life that you can. It should teach that natural laws are for your guidance, your fulfilment, your advantage and protection, your knowledge, and understanding, and your blessed joy. Creator wrote these laws within you; a) so that you could discover them and, b) that no one could overrule them. Nothing could be more objective than that.

Science is awakening to the importance of Man's individuated being, and to the interconnectedness of conscious and subconscious minds, as his spiritual essence. When Mans unalienable rights are truly honoured and protected, a voluntary, symbiotic community will follow. The more this path opens up, the easier it becomes.

What will smash this erroneous ideological conditioning, now centuries old? Nothing but conscious understanding, and action, will achieve it. That process is not automatic. Mental effort is needed. Free choice must activate it. Action must follow, or nothing is achieved.

Should we keep an open mind. Whoa! An open mind is part of the delusion! It allows all truth and fallacy without distinction. Open enquiry is valid. One searches for truth concerning one's life, that when found, cancels all that is not. Enquiry ceases, when truth releases. Knowledge results, belief having served its proper transitional purpose.

Ethics may be summed as objective, life-supporting evaluation, and judgement. Its prescriptions formulate the morality of our actions. Commitment to action follows, for which we as authors we are fully accountable.

Why has this simple explanation of life and natural laws escaped common knowledge, or academia for so long? Isn't the answer clear? Follow the money. Follow control. Escalate the principle. Switch ethics, and morality, from individuals to the collective, and control will multiply with ease. The ruse is extremely effective. Strip Man of personal values, so as to control the human species under the guise of accepted morality, and everyone's thoughts, and actions, are yours to determine, and rule. Man falls for this deceit, and has done so for centuries.

To become convinced of a higher power, and believe that it offers more, or that we can profit from its proclamations, we not only relinquish what we are, but forego much that we might achieve. Once we submit to a so-called *higher power*, which is all that government is, it may rule as it desires, including with violent force, while we're blind to the dynamic that permits it. Power brokers, know that their only power is yours, and that what you give them may control you.

Some people say, that your right to life, as a flesh and blood living being, has existed since homo sapiens emerged. That's a great thought, but it is fundamentally flawed. Its premise is that Man's rights apply collectively—that rights are born of society. Truth is different. Your (very own) right to life, began when you were born, not one millisecond before, and not one millisecond later. Prior that moment you were a (dependent) *potential* human being, subsequently an *actual* (independent) living being. Neither before, or after, were you ever a fictional legal entity. Neither did nature leave a window of opportunity, when you were born or at any time, for government to sneak in and declare you to be their chattel. Those who strip you of your right to life, have no such right, and no claim of right.

Much in this book challenges common acceptance and beliefs. My understanding was confronted many times during research and writing. *'Could this be true,'* I often asked myself. So I hunted for validation, evidence, correspondence, truthfulness, likeness, patterns of orders, sequence and flow. *'Don't give me a subjective opinion,'*

I pleaded. *'Give me pure, non-biased facts of life—because my life is indisputable fact!'* The works of Frank van Dun, philosopher of law, should not be overlooked. His understanding of this topic is profound.

24

DYNAMIC MAN

This book has spoken of a new paradigm for men, women, and children, founded on individual human life, as distinct from government rule based on *society by company*.

It is a sad fact, that modern law schools and most of their lawyers agree the notion that only *positive law* should count as law. So we are led to believe that it *is* law; despite it being nothing but an arbitrary collection of rules, defining a game, or a society. Society's orderliness only concerns personified positions, roles, and functions, today. Its success relies on rewards and punishments, that induce, or force natural living beings, to perform roles scripted for their *legal entity* to enact.

Law schools, and their disciples, should have identified the principles and patterns of order, pertaining to Man, and his social interactions in the human world. They did not. They sold out to a fiction-based *legal science*, and now force our compliance, in violation and contravention of natural law. The convivial order of natural living beings, is not merely dismissed without serious argument today, rather is rejected in full. That would undermine the fictional construct of *positive law,* and utterly destroy it, as it properly should.

Natural law, as here shown, stands in complete contrast. It represents a convivial order, or symbiotic society. Here, people interact as living beings, in accordance with the natural laws of their nature, regardless of any status, position, role, or function, in any social order to which they may belong. Conviviality is objective, and universal, the same at all times and place in any human population. No limit exists concerning possible goals, or schemes of such society, neither any limit by which one purpose, or plan of organisation can disband itself, perhaps to create a better replacement.

Before that is possible, one needs full understanding of the beautiful, and profound simplicity of natural laws, within oneself. They govern your life processes; permitting, and protecting. None command. None instruct. All uphold free will. You, are the master of your life, your destiny, and your soul. What data or information you choose to mentally process, is for your free will to decide.

Never before, have these laws been explained in this manner. None have explained the standpoint of orderliness. None have described the *triple sequential process,* presumably because no one sought to understand the relationship, or communion of conscious mind with subconscious mind.

- If you can grasp understanding of this finely governed process, that upholds and protects your life, even reporting its progress, and that you have unalienable right to choose what values you want to have upheld and protected, you will understand *Creator's invitation to live, like no other.*
- If you grasp likewise, that your right to life is protected, only by (you) upholding the right to life of all others, you will understand *Creator's invitation for friendly societies to develop and flourish.*

In principle, there is nothing more to learn but your nature and being, as the unique individual that you are! Agree that all others are equally independent, uphold their status in support of your own, and not one thing more is needed. Whatever controverts or violates this condition is unlawful; anti-life.

Full realisation will come from knowing what has been hidden, or not known, concerning Man's nature and his life, respective of the kind of society in which he should ideally live. Knowledge is of fundamental importance. Lies, and false ideologies, have no place. Truth matters, because one's life is the truth. Discernment and evaluation are critical.

It is sad that many new age fundamentalists have abandoned the word knowledge, instead, promoting beliefs, or belief systems. Many other examples can show how knowledge is denied, or circumvented. Little by little, over a long time span, Man has been stealthily forced to function in a state of animality, made servant to state without his knowing.

Let me make this observation very clear, by reprinting two (prior) statements, striking out the second, then adding a third.

1. Animals adapt themselves to nature, *as nature determines,*
2. ~~Man adapts nature to himself, (as free will determines),~~
3. Man adapts to the edicts of a state ruled society, *as its nature determines and enforces.*

Read 1 and 3 together. Man is reduced to animal status, by regulation, unknowingly. His life-force is struck out!

To reverse that condition, is today's ultimatum! If Man is to enjoy a future never dreamt of, he must learn to focus on his true being, not letting go of societal goals, but emphatically rejecting the (believed) necessity of a state to rule it.

Process that repeats is life

Life differentiates ethics from its lack, and morality from immorality.

- Thoughts, desires and goals that uphold one's life are *ethical*—those that do not, are not.
- Actions that respectfully uphold the lives of others are *moral*—those that do not, are not.

Ethics embrace one's private thoughts, intentions, and goals; affecting no one but oneself. Subsequently, they express as one's morality, or immorality, via one's actions. Today's task is to uphold the life of Man and his right to live it, to advocate and press for natural law. All legal fictions will fall in consequence. Unless study begins from the singularity of life and living, it has no relevance to any man woman or child. The non-aggression principle will follow, because it is within Creator's *natural law of no trespass.*

Human sciences have fallen short of identifying Mans natural processes, respective of life and its maintenance. They have dealt with attributes, and faculties, in isolation, leaving cooperative functioning aside. Conscious, and subconscious minds, may be thought of as individual beings, in a sense, but their full mental process is interactive. Their unity, cancels out complexity.

Let's recap. Perception of material things starts the mental process, by automatically integrating masses of sensory data. Secondly, we use (word) concepts to integrate incalculable volumes more information, so as to investigate, evaluate, and learn. Lastly, our emotional faculty assimilates vast sums of data to report progress instantaneously. Its automatic compass is beyond human comprehension.

These three, *perception, conceptual understanding,* and *progress summaries,* define the *sequential process,* as prior described. Mental stature grows through discernment, understanding, knowledge, wisdom, and values. Ethical choices result in moral actions, while feelings, being one's mentoring reports, advise progress or its lack. Beginning with the five senses, that's the clockwise path shown in diagram 16.

For each additional circuit, starting each time at (1), we have new perceptions to consider, along with mentoring reports from past actions. As each new cycle comes around, and is learned from, so discernment, understanding, knowledge, wisdom, and values grow exponentially. That path is from left to right in diagram 16. Intuition kicks in automatically, to simplify mental processing even further.

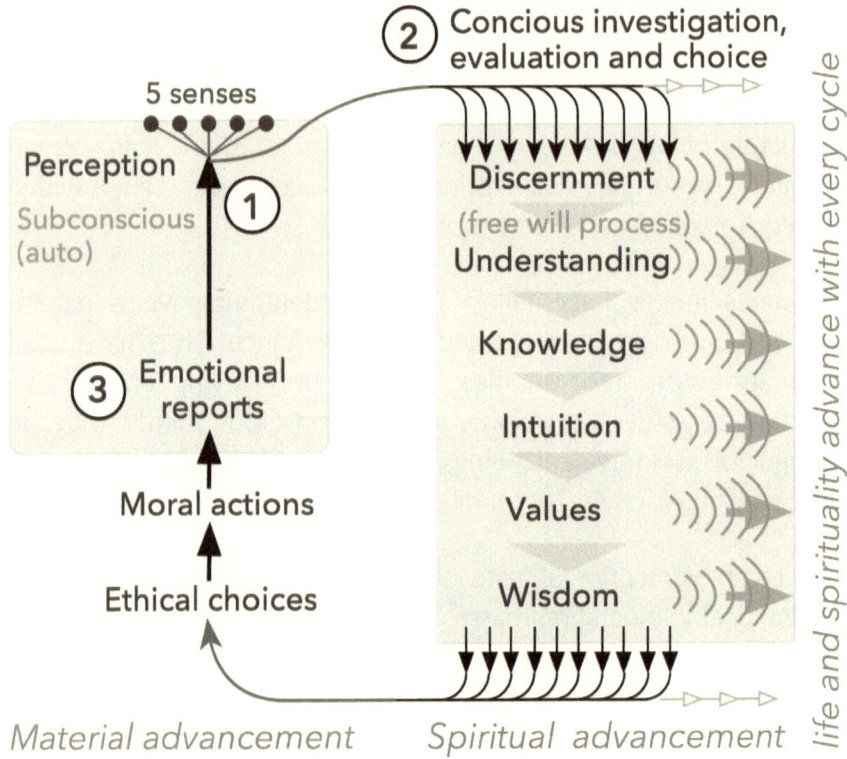

16 - Repeating cycles advance life

What first seems enormously complex, is a (single) repeating process. Beautiful simplicity lies in the process repeating over and over, for the course of one's life. Each repetition of it builds understanding, knowledge, intellectual, and spiritual growth, all united in service of life.

That simplicity, and that natural orderliness is not understood today. Consequently, natural law is left unexplained, unavailable for translation into ethics, morality, or a free and just society. No one sees Creator's invitation for all men, women, and children to live a bountifully joyful, and rewarding life. No one understands, how natural laws ensure that you can. Few grasp how these laws, in very simple form, can teach children about ethical, and moral thinking from a very early age.

How can people comprehend the consequences of not abiding natural law and respecting it, when they've no idea it actually exists? Man's bloody, tragic, psychopathic, warmongering history is evidential proof of what he has failed to learn, and employ to massive advantage.

Who suffers, and who gains, when every living being is effectively forced to focus on the state's complex legalities, backed by (gunpowder) rules? Who suffers, and to what degree, when needless legal inventions drain the life and soul, out of every person, so creating huge mental problems and traumas? Who profits, when our mental capacity is needlessly overburdened and diverted? Are we to put freedom aside, leave corrupt ideologies in the *too-hard basket*, forget unceasing tyranny, and lift our game by simply meditating, or *raising our consciousness*?

Who profits, when the populace screams *government must do something!* Who suffers when it does?

Given this interminable, oppressive environment, how could anyone possibly conceive of a lawful, friendly, supportive, and cooperative *society,* based on natural laws offering freedom and security; one in which protection is offered by trespasser's, whose actions self-confess violation of natural law?

Reciprocal autonomy

To understand natural law, is to comprehend the fullness and beauty of oneself; not mankind, government, statute laws, positive law, or society! It is to comprehend, that when Creator ordained Mans free choice to live life to the fullest imaginable, *natural laws must concretely ensure it.*

Nature guarantees that one's mental choices can never corrupt the vital mental processes; reciprocally ensuring that mental processes can never override one's free options. Each had to be guaranteed autonomy so as to contribute to the other, cooperatively and harmoniously without interference. That left free will to be free.

What better explanation sums individuality, individual rights and natural law than Creator's testament of all three. There is no better example of the principle of non-aggression; none! It is Creator's *natural law of no trespass.* No better societal model has ever offered—but institution of individual rights is the only thing that can grant it!

Few advocates of the non-aggression principle (NAP) understand this totality, or its source. The *natural laws of independence, equality, integrity, individual rights, and free will,* are all contained within the *natural law of no trespass. Commitment, allowance and respect* are inclusive, ethics and morality also. This lesson is profound; never to be overstated. Man's nature and his life, are the bottom line; the only adjudicator of his rights, and any social structures that he may desire.

Some argue that only three laws exist—keep the peace, love others as oneself, and respect free will causing no harm or trespass—or words to that effect. All are true in societal principle, but lack substantive qualification. None define one's self, one's inalienable right to life, what constitutes free will, how harm, or trespass is caused, and by whom, or what constitutes natural justice.

Will anything change, while the agreed mindset holds tight to the notion that society prevails above all; to which individual men and women must be a servant; animal status or not?

Does Mans ignorance of natural law result from mental apathy, ignorance concerning his faculties, blind acceptance of *collectivism,* whose social structure enforces compliance with deadly force, or all three? If (sociopathic) *rulers,* could conspire to conceal Mans true individuality, and force authoritarian rule as law, intentionally making Man slave without his knowing, why would they not? Ignorance, and servility, thus taught and ingrained into Mans consciousness, would cement authoritarian rule, domination, and control, forever, wouldn't it? Isn't history that proof? Should it surprise, that Man regularly votes for this criminal continuance the world over, and no one ever asks *'by what God-given right?'*

Today's task is to advocate, build, and practice individual rights. Pull the foundation from under authority, and sociopathic dominance over Man will crash.

The very purposeful reason, why the *Constitution of Man* is more than three simple petitions, is to offset simplistic inadequacy. Any document that upholds Mans life, must express that every violator self-confesses unlawful trespass. If not, then its (constitutional) substance fails natural law, that in turn fails mankind.

Creator has allowed every man and woman to disagree *'nature and nature's God'* as Thomas Jefferson's so succinctly phrased. Everyone is permitted to flaunt, or violate natural law, and Man's life, according to their free choice. While so doing, amounts to spitting in Creator's face, outlaws will reap what they sow. Natural justice will prevail despite all our evasions, as Mans entire history testifies, and continues to prove. Innocent victims are not collateral damage, they are proof of gross criminality.

Justness

If you fully understand what you've just read, and it brings the phrase *natural justice* to mind, then *your understanding of natural law* is virtually unsurpassable! You've totally *got it.* You've fully grasped, that not one cell, or organ in Man's body can outrage another while both support one's life. You've fully grasped, that conscious mind can influence the content of the subconscious mind but cannot overrule its process. Correspondingly that subconscious mind can (emotionally) report to conscious mind, but cannot overrule its process. You fully understand the moral principle that one man or woman cannot violate another, while supporting the concept of life in societal terms. You fully accept that every action, that violates life, self *confesses an act of violation*. So you have grasped the full essence of *criminal law.*

You perfectly understand that all body and mental processes, must *justly* deliver from one to the other, or they violate the life which they professedly uphold. From this understanding you've grasped the vital essence of *contract law.* Justice, under natural law, involves the following, generally insofar as actions are concerned.

- No such thing as a victimless crime exists.
- Justice allows that all charges be made transparent and public, for all to see.
- Justice allows all evidence to be made public.
- Justice allows the accuser, and accused, to testify openly and in public, such that much healing can take place from the telling of one's story, while jurors and others listen with objective, reflective, and compassionate intent.
- Justice allows the accused opportunity to confess, repent, or express regret, offer restitution, and be forgiven if agreed. It allows the accuser, to accept and offer forgiveness.
- Rehabilitation for the offender is allowed if required.
- Justice requires that where court procedures, and jury deliberations continue, they do so openly and publicly.
- If charged, to offer the accused a formal opportunity to confess, repent, offer remediation, to be forgiven publicly.
- Where an offender refuses all offers of restoration, and/or repeats the offence, detainment or imprisonment would likely result.

I've assembled these qualifications from my research, and conclusions that follow. Those who work in law, and the legal professions, may take them further. That may require a great mental leap on their part, but if you've understood the explanations here, then you've already made a huge leap in understanding law, respective of a convivial, symbiotic society.

No individual can violate another, without confessing violation of life by that action.

- One acts justly, or in justness when one's actions uphold life.
- One acts unjustly, or without justness, when one's actions violate life, whether of self or others.

A free symbiotic society will defend that one's life choices can never corrupt the necessary (right to life) processes of another. Do this, and a free society is the only possible outcome; save unlawful interference! Your life is truthful proof of this concept, absolutely.

The natural law now comes alive in the social arena. Most all of Mans twenty natural laws, previously described, concern personal ethics. Today's choice is clear cut. If Man wishes to accept natural law and Creator's invitation to live true to nature, then all *artificial* law must be abolished. If not, one's right to life cancels, men and women are kept slave to fake legalities, while the whole criminal mess is hailed morally lawful. Nothing better emphasises the *Natural Law of Just Consequence;* reap what you sow.

Adaptation

Increasingly, people are awakening to the realisation that society is not serving their real nature. Some consider *awakening,* as expanding their consciousness, or raising their vibrations. Others believe we need to return to the (US) Constitution. Others foresee a spiritual transformation, while others hold out for a global currency reset, a return to the gold standard, a disclosure of extraterrestrial beings, critical mass for worldwide ascension, etcetera. Others want a political, or legal re-ordering, e.g., return to common law. What, we might ask, do all these *awakenings* have in common? What, exactly, is triggering these motivations for a change? Is it mere dissatisfaction, or is there something greater? Some say there are energies at play. Others talk of a unity consciousness, that supposedly we can rise to, or embrace.

There may be elements of truth in all the above, but none answer why Mankind's revival is steadily increasing. There is a real reason, I submit, one that human society has never before experienced. I refer to the information explosion, made available through the internet. Truth, along with every bogus philosophy, and ideology ever invented, is available to far greater numbers than ever before. In little more than two decades, dialogue has exploded, through email, SMS, video, podcasts, e-books, and blog sites. This outpouring of information, allows people greater means to employ it in their lives, to test hypotheses, compare results with others, concur, experiment, evaluate and learn.

But what exactly are these folk learning? What truth? How much remains as beliefs, false ideological acceptance, or restated mystical revelations? How many so called *energy vibrations* premise on the collective, and not individuals? These are all vital questions. If what people are accepting and absorbing, is nothing but a (modern day) rehash of ideologies that never did work, and can never serve their needs, then dissatisfaction is undoubtedly multiplied by wider dissemination. Demand for solutions increases, but satisfactions do not, accounting for more soul searching, with still wider disparity, as above.

Awakening, in the strict sense of that description, is not the measure of progress, I submit, but lack thereof. Does today's thirst for *awakening,* show real evidence of it being found? Are we truthfully discovering the reality of life, or gullibly swallowing centuries-old ideologies, dished up in modern day phraseology that sounds plausible, comforting, and benignly assuring?

Are we looking to the nature of Man himself, which is where any right thinking person would expect an *awakening* to take place? Or are we falling for the same misguided philosophies that have tortured Man over centuries past, dressed up in sheep's clothing, or fancy new age vocabulary?

Are we searching for societal answers, bogged down by externalities, prejudices, and age-old notions, or are we truly focussed on who and what we truly are as individuals? For, surely as Mankind considers that social order is superior to, or outside his own, he will accept answers to his enquiries based on that mindset. If supposed solutions, or awakening, are externally oriented, and not internal, then who, exactly, has *awakened*; who, or what profits?

Law from within

Epistemology is the theory of knowledge, especially concerning its methods, validity, and scope. Some adhere to an epistemology based on life, and reality, for their guidance. Others do not. Differences, and (seeming) contradictions can arise. These point to errors in thinking, or evidence needing correction, because contradictions cannot exist in reality.

Caterpillars, who find freedom like a butterfly, will never learn of the total change in every aspect of their existence, but if Man is to become free, he must know how to order it.

Life will change in ways never expected, often barely imaginable. Those whose values call them to reason in harmony with nature, and reality, despite differences, will ultimately reach the same conclusions—different train tracks to the same destination. They will prize their respect for concepts and integrated thinking, never allowing corrupted language, or meanings. Fully understanding the *laws of identity, and causality,* they relish consistency, non-contradiction, syllogisms, and principles. Vital necessity, to definitively use basic words like freedom, slavery, theft, coercion, fraud, morality, justness, and justice, is paramount to their success, and their achievements. They will rid themselves from TV mind programming, and indoctrination by media. Then, as more and still more people wake up to this manifest simplicity, and utilise it, so the reign of tyranny will end.

- This book has challenged collectivist conditioning, and many more commonly accepted tenets.
- It has presented evidence that every man woman and child is an individual, and that all understanding of Man's nature is thus; not collectively founded. Almost every philosophy, theology, and ideology, is called into question thereby.
- It has presented evidence, that every man, woman and child, has a *triple sequential process* that repeats. This revelation alone, challenges almost every human science, including those dealing with Mans six higher faculties.
- Two-way communication, between conscious and subconscious mind, has offered Man as a *spiritual being* living a *spiritual life* within a p*hysical environment*. This position challenges volumes of thought on this topic, much common belief, and most all religion.
- Man's unalienable right to life, and his inalienable right to property, *retrieve individual rights from the political arena;* thus overturning all present understanding of human rights, per the (world acclaimed) UDHR document.
- This book offers, that *one who upholds the rights of all others to their life, automatically defends his own.* No other assurance can match this accomplishment. (It's not the non-aggression principle; it's *the right to life principle*.)
- Twenty natural laws emerge, all stemming from process governance within Mans physical, mental, and emotional being. None command free will choice. All uphold Mans

life. Thus natural law comes from within every man, woman, and child.

- These natural laws may directly merge into a free, symbiotic society, verbatim. No alteration is needed. Once achieved, none will command free will choice, rather all will uphold Mans individuated life, and his right to live it.
- Together these laws underwrite a science of ethics, for all men and women, one that children can absorb from a very young age. How can a science of ethics apply to all men and women if it comes from within each? It is because we are all equal in nature, but different in expression.
- Ethics is thought bound, while actions demonstrate morality, or its lack. Each living being is the author of their actions, and justly accountable for them.
- Whosoever trespasses natural law, by violating another's right to life, is not free; indeed self-confesses immorality, and violation of natural law. (Government has no exception— every operative a living human being, with free choice and full accountability.) People unwilling to live and act, according to natural law, are obliged to accept *just consequences*.
- Justice concerns remediation of trespass, respectful of its causal action(s).

All the above is upheld by the Constitution *of* Man— not a Constitution *for* Man—reasons being that law is from within. The document underscores Mans equalit in all countries, cultures, and religions, as never before presented.

We now have opportunity to entirely divorce from societal domination and control, that has damnably beleaguered Mans entire history. Will this raise Mans consciousness? No. It is perfect, just as Creator endowed it. That considered, Man will learn to use it fully. Once understood that value assessments should be impressed on the subconscious mind, whereby one's (emotional) mentoring system will report in exact accord with one's choices, mental emancipation will skyrocket. No better mentoring system exists; notifications appear in milliseconds. Self-mastery will be vividly transparent to those who choose to practice it!

Once understood on a wide scale how beneficial this practice is, and how efficiently it may be done, all forms of domination and control will fail, regardless of promised (faux) benefits. In a symbiotic society, vacant ideologies, religious persuasions, and legal fictions will die from lack of support.

Dynamic man

Past chapters have offered a new focus for all Mankind; one of integrity, beauty, simplicity and spirituality. That Man must adapt material nature to his spiritual nature, is what I want you to treasure above all else—as though your life depended on it—because it does!

Whoever sets this goal, and accomplishes it to a masterful degree, (perfection unnecessary), may be described as a dynamic man, or woman. These individuals conquer their environment by first mastering their body and minds. They grasp the essence of the *sequential process,* even though they may know little of its method and sequences. They attune to spiritual values, and utilise them as lifestyles necessities, whereafter worldly material values fall neatly into line. So they are enabled to influence their life, in a manner far greater than what had previously demanded their submission. Dynamic men and women know, and relish, that they are the term setters of their life. Their life is theirs! They choose how things are to be. They determine how material existence will serve their spiritual needs and desires, according to their judgements and their values.

Dynamic men and women understand their equality with all others, and their separate uniqueness. They know, that their personal life is the baseline reference in all matters and all decisions. Hence they respect themselves, and all others jointly, always upholding the right to life. They understand strengths and weaknesses, in themselves and others, and how the *laws of allowance, efficacy, free will, integrity and just consequence* affect both. Consequently, they fully understand that open collaboration with others, is one of the most beneficial forms of adaptation available. Cooperative enterprise opens opportunities for material, and spiritual advancement, like no other. For this reason, if no other, they grasp the vital importance of *value education* in very impressionable young minds; most especially their offspring. They live each moment like a child, full of wonderment and curiosity, fully attuned to all blessings and demands of nature; their own most particularly.

These dynamic folk make no demands, save upon their individual integrity, values, honesty, truth, and respect for others. They accept all responsibility, and accountability, for their actions. They accept no authority, and they issue none. They seek not to amend *positive law,* to return to the Constitution, or to institute the *common law,* because the natural law suffices in all respects; all else irrelevant. Setting their desires and ambitions, their objectives and values on Mans nature and life, they rightfully, and lawfully establish, that any and all who challenge Man's precedent right to life, should refer their dispute to Creator.

Dynamic men and women understand the most humble fullness, and exactness, in saying, 'I am.'

'I am'

The short novel, *Anthem,* by Ayn Rand, published in 1938, deals with professed values of our entire civilisation. The central character, Equality 7-2521, begins a process of self-discovery, and self-fulfillment, that cogently expresses the difference between a collectivist society, and a friendly society founded on individual self, its rights, and autonomy. Held captive by forced domination, and control, he escapes. Prior taught to think, and speak of himself as *we,* tears of deliverance flow when he discovers the word '*I.*' His full understanding of the phrase, '*I am,*' leads to his profound understanding of how humans are stripped of their nature. In books found after his escape, he learns that individuals live with immutable right to pursue their happiness, in freedom, never to be enslaved by any group. So he proclaims—

> I know not if this earth on which I stand is the core of the universe or if it is but a speck of dust lost in eternity. I know not and I care not. For I know what happiness is possible to me on earth. And my happiness needs no higher aim to vindicate it. My happiness is not a means to any end. It is the end. It is its own goal. It is its own purpose.
>
> Neither am I the means to any end others may wish to accomplish. I am not a tool for their use. I am not a servant of their needs. I am not a bandage on their wounds. I am not a a sacrifice on their altars.
>
> I am a man. —Ayn Rand [xix]

Anthem is about us; an incredibly powerful expose of fascist slavery, with freedom its counterpoint. It most poignantly expresses that which the author had hoped Man would soon avert. Namely, at the crossroads of his consciousness, come to his senses, fully understand what fails his life, and what redeems it. Has that time now come, 79 years after its publication? What will you choose, for yourself, and your children?

- Continued reliance on commonly accepted, but failed ideologies that foster criminally mastered (legal) slavery, based on Man as a social animal? Or—
- Creator's invitation to live in full accordance with natural laws, in freedom, and in peace, with your unalienable right to choose your course, and purpose in life?

Will you allow others to decide who you are, and whom you must serve —or will you proclaim 'I AM?'

****

The next chapter presents a *document*, so to speak, (format) styled on the 1776 united states of America's *Declaration of Independence,* even bearing some of the same phrases. Thomas Jefferson later admitted, that the *Declaration* served all Mankind, not Americans alone. In honour of his intentions, what follows, departs from the 1776 original document, in that instead of listing grievances for divorce, it lists achievable triumphs that freedom makes possible. As a bold, authentic statement of *I AM,* it declares that 'I,' and all men and women, are by their nature and life, unequivocally and eternally free from all artificial order, all men and women free from authority, and state, no dispute save to *'nature and nature's God.'*

25

PRIVATE DECLARATION OF INDEPENDENCE

Self-evident truth, holds all Men created equal in nature, while unique in expression, endowed by their Creator with certain rights, among which life, liberty, and the pursuit of happiness, are immutable and unalienable. Natural law within all men and women, is beyond self-evident, axiomatic by nature; all personal, societal, and business dealings achievable, correspondent with unalienable,individual rights, rightful freedom, and unobstructed action within our will, drawn around us by the equal rights of all others.

Notwithstanding, false and misleading theologies, ideologies, and philosophies, have hidden, perverted, misconstrued, and overruled nature's laws, and Man's right to life, as though non-existent. Blinded, deluded,, and deceived, Man is branded a social animal, made slave to political society with no disclosure. Forbidden redress by immoral, legal rules, artifice, corruption, and criminality in defiance of a free people, and unalienable right to life, Man is insanely forced to uphold bloody-minded tyranny, as the only liberty possible!

When legislations constrain men, and women, contrary to their nature, by any fictional or covert invention, when criminal abuse, usurpations, and violation of Mans right to life, reduce existence to animal-like status under absolute despotism, cessation of insufferable, criminal evil, demands. When injuries, violence, and usurpations, consistently repeat for the direct object of tyranny over Man, so its indisputable criminality, summed as *'moral right to rule'* and *'immoral wrong to refuse rule,'* is historical fact—open to all seekers of truth—no need to re-state it.

Accepting equality, and individual station entitled by the laws of nature, and Creator, it is men and women's unalienable right, indeed their duty as living beings, to abolish all legislations, entirely divorce from criminal, and unjust legal authority. Each, and all of the One People of Earth, impelled to determine full separation, and independence from all (state) power and rule, backed by force, now seek to institute, and secure new protections in perpetuity, deriving just powers from those endowed by Creator—the laws of nature and nature's God.

In full absolution, of centuries-old criminal violation of Man's right to life, let the (natural) laws of nature and Creator, be openly submitted to a candid world, for the lawful upholding of human life, contrary every criminality, abomination, defilement, and violation. To that effect—

1. Natural law, (Law), is the natural order of human beings, capable of rational, purposive action, speech and thought, the natural order of the human world, expressing method, system, process, order, equality, uniqueness, all inviting of free choice, within free and cooperative rightful action.
2. All men, and women, of Homo sapiens as species, possess like faculty, (governed thought processes), in union with certain free expression, (independent free will thoughts), irrefutably testifying all living beings equal, independently free, and complete in nature—*mankind* their aggregation—not collection.
3. Independent faculty is guaranteed, inclusive of individual responsibility, liability, and accountability; actioned consequences inescapable. Respect for the lives of others,

reciprocally ensures one's own, never sacrificing life's supreme value to anything lesser.

4. Individual right to life, is unalienable right to the action of living, the faculties of movement, feeling, thought, and speech, without usurping, or violating the unalienable rights of any other.

5. Where the rights of all others are respected, no one can offend by any application of his own.

6. The right to act in support of life, is unalienable; the right to the product of one's efforts is inalienable.

7. Individual rights preside over all other life forms, and preclude collective rights.

8. To secure the certain unalienable right to life, unless all men created equal, unequivocally protect their right to life, and their unalienable right so to do, against all violation, cancellation or usurpation, they will have neither.

9. No authority, is granted any individual to command another. Likewise, all commandment is refused, no man or woman a human agent. No legal, or other instrument may preside contrary.

10. All thoughts and intentions are self-contained; unable to violate another's right to life or property.

11. Conversely, actions, and behaviour that violate another's right to life—when proven—publicly confess immorality, immoral action(s) and trespass of natural law. Fraud, blackmail, rape, theft and murder do not occur accidentally.

12. Actioned trespass of natural law, admits to its lawful cessation, agreement to remediate harm and endure restoration, respectful of that transgression.

13. Criminal action forfeits freedom, rightful justice remedially acquired by the victim, without which, no rights and no freedoms can exist.

14. Natural justice binds. Because free society and natural law are co-dependent, each must guarantee non-violation of the other, or both vanish.

Natural laws of perfected self-governing, are the *'separate and equal station to which the laws of nature and nature's God entitle each man and woman.'* Perfectly modelled for verbatim transfer into Mans societies, so decent respect for natural law declares separation from all contrary, all men and women from the state, Creator's natural laws of proven and perfected societal governing commissioned forthwith.

By nature thus endowed, we do, with full rectitude, solemnly publish, and declare, that all men and women are by their nature and life, unequivocally and eternally free from all artificial order; all men and women free from authority, and state, no dispute save to *'nature and nature's God.'*

With firm, and resolute reliance on the steadfast integrity and protection of *Source*, I, in this moment, pledge my sacred honour to my fellow men and women, that within my immutable right to life, and its protections, humbly make this my solemn, *private, Declaration of Independence.*

Autograph this _____ day of _____ _____

Witness   this _____ day of _____ _____

ABOUT THE AUTHOR

Kenneth's upbringing on a dairy farm, taught resilience, independence, and self-sufficiency. From 22 years old, he has used the principles of *objectivist philosophy*, because, *they work*. Short adventures in electrical, mechanical, and structural engineering, gave way to a career in residential architecture, and sustainable design. Much work concerned research, writing of building contracts, and legal town-planning documents, three employers being attorneys. These disciplines came together, as a pioneer solar house designer, over twenty-eight years in Western Australia. Since his retirement, much public dissatisfaction with governments, begged the question of alternatives. Some spoke of natural law, but none objectively described it. Kenneth seized this opportunity, choosing Man's individual life as his focus, not society, or government. As enquiries deepened, natural law united with objectivist philosophy. Thorough understanding, sprang forth to become this book. Today Kenneth lives on the Coffs Coast, in New South Wales. Photography his hobby, he writes about freedom, individual rights, and natural law. Discussions concerning the source of natural law are scarce, although known for centuries past. Kenneth's understanding of its totality is unprecedented; his *'Constitution of Man,'* and *'Private Declaration of Independence,'* aided by proposal for a *'Commission of Justice,'* are unique, all standing proudly on the world stage.

BIBLIOGRAPHY

i   van Dun, Frank. "The Lawful and the legal" Web address, http://users. ugent.be/~frvandun/Texts/Articles/The%20Lawful%20and%20the%20 Legal.html

ii   Griffith, Jeremy. "The Book of Real Answers to Everything", Web address, Jeremy Griffith https://www.humancondition.com/book-of-real-answers/

iii   Griffith, Jeremy. "Biologist Jeremy Griffith examines where the human race is headed." Web address, http://www.smh.com.au/national/education/ biologist-jeremy-griffith-examines-where-the-human-race-is-headed-20141006-10qyvm.html

iv   The Bible, "King James version." Web address, https://www.kingjames bibleonline.org/1-Corinthians-13-11/

v   Rand, Ayn. "Ayn Rand Lexicon." "Subconscious." Web address, http:// aynrandlexicon.com/lexicon/subconscious.html

vi   Grohol, John M, Psy.D. "Humans are governed by emotions." Web address, http://psychcentral.com/blog/archives/2005/10/20/humans-are-governed-by-emotions/

vii   Sydney Morning Herald. "Shock discovery in Economic Man's Mind." Web address, http://www.smh.com.au/articles/2004/04/11/1081621834674. html?from=storyrhs

viii   van Dun, Frank. "Natural Rights." Web address, http://users.ugent.be/ ~frvandun/Texts/Logica/NaturalLaw2.htm

ix   Rand, Ayn. "Ayn Rand Lexicon." "Individual Rights." Web address, http:// aynrandlexicon.com/lexicon/individual_rights.html

x   Adask, Alfred. "Unalienable vs Inalienable." Web address, https://adask. wordpress.com/2009/07/15/unalienable-vs-inalienable/

xi   Rand, Ayn. "Ayn Rand Lexicon." "Property rights." Web address, http:// aynrandlexicon.com/lexicon/property_rights.html

xii   Rand, Ayn. "Rights." Web address, http://tradingsuccess.com/blog/wp-content/uploads/2016/03/man-rights.pdf

xiii   Rand, Ayn. "Ayn Rand Lexicon." "Physical Force" http://aynrandlexicon. com/lexicon/physical_force.html

xiv   Spooner, Lysander. "Natural Law." –"The Science of Justice." Web address, https://www.scribd.com/document/155601745/INGLES-Spooner-Natural-Law-or-the-Science-of-Justice-pdf

xv   Blackstone, William. "William Blackstone Quotes." Web address, http://www.azquotes.com/author/1461-William_Blackstone

xvi   van Dun, Frank. "Kritarchy', an article by Frank van Dun" Web address, https://americankritarchists.wordpress.com/article-by-frank-van-dun/

xvii   Website. Secrets of the Fed.com. "Spain is without a national government and the people are loving it." Web address, http://secretsofthefed.com/spain-is-without-a-national-government-and-the-people-are-loving-it/

xviii   Website. Anarchism.net. "Manifesto." Web address, http://www.anarchism.net/warren-manifesto.htm

xix   Rand, Ayn. "Anthem," Create SpacePublishing, Barnes and Noble, Web address, http://www.barnesandnoble.com/w/anthem-ayn-rand/1116684471

www.ingramcontent.com/pod-product-compliance
Lightning Source LLC
Chambersburg PA
CBHW030425290526
45786CB00001B/142